Made for His Purpose

How to Find Your Place in God's Plan

By Dr. Tony Williams

The Divine Design Series

Made for His Purpose: How to Find Your Place in God's Plan
©2018 Dr. Tony Williams

ISBN: 97-80986134777

All rights reserved.

No part of this publication may be reproduced, distributed, or transmitted in any form or by any means, including photocopying, recording, or other electronic or mechanical methods, without the prior written permission of the publisher, except in the case of brief quotations embodied in critical reviews and certain other noncommercial uses permitted by copyright law.

Cover design by Susanne Lakin and Ellie Searl. Edited by Susanne Lakin.

Scripture quotations marked "ESV" are from the ESV Bible® (The Holy Bible, English Standard Version®), copyright by Crossway Bibles, a publishing ministry of Good News Publishers. Used by permission. All rights reserved.

Scripture quotations marked "KJV" are taken from the Holy Bible, King James Version

Scripture quotations marked "NASB" are taken from the New American Standard Bible®, Copyright © 1960, 1962, 1963, 1968, 1971, 1972, 1973, 1975, 1977, 1995 by The Lockman Foundation. Used by permission.

Scripture quotations marked (NIV) are taken from the Holy Bible, New International Version®, NIV®. Copyright © 1973, 1978, 1984 by Biblica, Inc.™ Used by permission of Zondervan. All rights reserved worldwide.

Scripture quotations marked "NKJV" are taken from the New King James Version. Copyright © 1982 by Thomas Nelson, Inc. Used by permission. All rights reserved.

Scripture quotations marked (NLT) are taken from the Holy Bible, New Living Translation, copyright © 1996, 2004, 2007 by Tyndale House Foundation. Used by permission of Tyndale House Publishers, Inc., Carol Stream, Illinois 60188.

Scripture quotations marked "NRSV" are taken from the New Revised Standard Version Bible, copyright 1989, Division of Christian Education of the National Council of the Churches of Christ in the United States of America. Used by permission. All rights reserved.

Scripture quotations marked "MSG" or "The Message" are taken from The Message. Copyright 1993, 1994, 1995, 1996, 2000, 2001, 2002. Used by permission of NavPress Publishing Group.

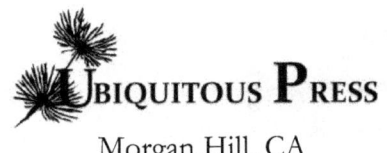

Morgan Hill, CA

Table of Contents

Introduction: Your Divine Design 1
   Chapter 1: Our Four "Relationships" with Christ 5

The First "P" – Person 9
   Chapter 2: God Is the One Who Defines Us 10
   Chapter 3: God Defines Our Identity 21
   Chapter 4: Relationship Is the Key to Our Identity 31

The Second "P" – Position 41
   Chapter 5: Know Your Place 42

The Third "P" – Purpose 57
   Chapter 6: Letting God Define Our Purpose 58
   Chapter 7: God Bestows Gifts 67
   Chapter 8: Seven Pillars of Wisdom 74

The Fourth "P" – Performance 79
   Chapter 9: God's Purpose Leads to Performance 80

The Fifth "P" – Product 85
   Chapter 10: Produce Much Fruit 86

The Sixth "P" – Praise 95
   Chapter 11: The Praises Go Up 96

The Seventh "P" – Presence 103
   Chapter 12: Oh, to Be in His Presence 104

About the Author 111

Introduction: Your Divine Design

Have you ever tried to picture all the billions of people living on earth at any given moment? It's hard enough just imagining a hundred people in a crowd and seeing every face and noting the unique differences of each person. Much harder to conjure a million . . . ten million . . . six thousand million.

We shake our heads and wonder: How does God see each and every person? How does He know us all individually—and not just by name but every tiny thing about us, from the number of atoms in our body to the hairs on our head?

When we look at the extreme diversity in nature—not just those billions of unique people covering the face of the earth but the countless species of birds, insects, mammals, and fish—it's easy to feel insignificant. Yet, the Bible says the Creator of the earth also knows the names of every star and that He put each in its place—and there are said to be billions of stars, not one exactly like the other, just as snowflakes and the grains of sand in a desert are individually unique (Isa. 40:26).

We're so much smaller than any star, but the Bible tells us God values us. "You have made [man] a little lower than the heavenly beings and crowned him with glory and honor" (Psalm 8:5 ESV). This Creator of the vast universe knew us before we were formed in the womb and watched our bones knit together. And, more astounding than that, He saw our entire life spread out before Him before we were even conceived. The psalmist wrote: "Every day of my life was recorded in your book. Every moment was laid out before a single day had passed" (Psalm 139:15–16 NLT).

Does that amaze you? It should. For it means that God has designed us all with a purpose. But not just any general purpose—a *specific, unique* purpose. Ephesians 2:10 (NLT) says: "For we are God's masterpiece. He has created us anew in Christ Jesus, so we can do the good things he planned for us long ago."

In the heavenly kingdom, God has given general as well as specific designs for each person's life. By understanding how and why God designed *you*, you will come to know your specific purpose in life and how to "walk" that out. You can come to know the "good things" God has for you. "For *I know* the plans I have for you," God says, "plans to prosper you and not to harm you, plans to give you hope and a future" (Jer. 29:11 NIV).

Just as everything in nature serves the purpose God intended, through understanding the person of God and His intent for your life, you will see how you fit into divine design and find fulfillment in your place in this vast universe.

7 P's to Help You Find Your Place in God's Plan

What this book will be covering are the seven "Particular P's" that go into your divine design. Seven facets that tell you who you are and who God designed you to be. Let's take a brief look at what those are before we delve deeply into each one.

1. Person: The first "P" that goes into your divine design is your *Person*. Your identity. In order to understand your divine design, you must understand who you are—your personality, gifts, abilities, strengths, weaknesses—all that and more.

2. Position: The second "P" is your *Position*. That is, your place in Him and your place in His will. We must position ourselves so that God can do exactly what He has purposed and designed to do in our lives.

3. Purpose: What is purpose? It's our destiny, our calling. What it is that God has gifted us to do. The will of God for our lives. And discovering and fulfilling that purpose is so important because real success in ministry, real success in life, and real success in your relationship with Christ comes from you fulfilling the purpose of God.

And it is not as difficult as you may think. But it is important that we understand the purpose of God. For if you do not have a clear purpose in life, you will face great difficulty making the right choices and decisions.

4. Performance: Once we understand our purpose, we must *Perform* our purpose. That's our service. "Well done" is better than "well said."

It's one thing to know that God has called you to do something with your life, but it's a whole other thing to *perform* that purpose—that's where the rubber meets the road.

5. Product: Once we have performed the purpose of God, there is a *Product*—the fruit produced in our lives. The end of the assembly line of our life must produce something of value. Jesus said, "By this my Father is glorified, that you bear much fruit" (John 15:8 NKJV). The first words God ever spoke to a man were "Be fruitful and multiply" (Gen. 1:22).

God is after a people that will be productive for the kingdom, productive in their own lives. And so, when we perform our purpose, there is a product that is produced.

6. Praise: That product that is produced then brings *Praise* to God. "By this my Father is glorified." God is glorified when we raise our hands, when we sing, when we worship, and when we give Him praise and honor and glory. But He receives the greatest glory by the fruit we produce. In essence, Jesus says, "You really want to know how to glorify the Father? Bear much fruit."

There is a difference between coming to church, raising our hands, and singing songs and being fruitful. What do we offer to the Lord? When we are told to continually praise the Lord, and that our praise for Him should be "continually" in our mouths (Psalm 34:1), does that mean that we go around all day saying, "Praise the Lord . . . Praise the Lord . . . Praise the Lord . . ."?

You've met people that do that. They say, "How are you doing? Praise the Lord, Brother." Right? "Praise the Lord! The Lord told me to come and praise the Lord! How am I doing? Praise the Lord." That is not what God means. Yes, there is a time when it's wholly appropriate to express worship and praise with the lifting of our hands and voices, but there is also worship as the *product* of our lives. We are created in Him to *be* a praise *to* Him. And when we are productive, what we produce brings praise to God.

7. *Presence:* And finally, what is our end goal in praising God? To bestow worship. And when we worship Him, we evoke His *Presence*. Our destination is the presence of God. The Bible noted back in the early days of the Israelites that God inhabited the praises of His people (Psalm 22:3). The Hebrew word *yashab* used in this verse implies *dwelling within, to remain, stay, have one's abode*.

This is not a quick rest stop that God takes with us and then He moves on. Being in His presence means He reigns in our life, enthroned in the praises of His people—in our praises. And that's what we want, after all—the presence of God.

That is what I'm after. That is what I want more than anything. I want Him inhabiting my praises, and I want my life to give forth praise. That should be our goal and our desire— Him. God doesn't inhabit our praises as a result of continually exalting Him in worship, although He welcomes such "sacrifices" of praise. Rather, He inhabits our praises because our lives are continually fruitful by fulfilling His purpose for our lives.

Chapter 1: Our Four "Relationships" with Christ

At the heart of purpose, of understanding how we are made for God's purpose, is our relationship to His Son, Christ Jesus. Apart from Him, we can do nothing (John 15:5). Our lives have no value, no worth, apart from Jesus. Everything in heaven and on earth was made through Him, by Him, and for Him (John 1:3; Colossians 1:16).

In order to understand, accept, and fulfill who we are in Christ—understand our Identity or "Person" —we need to look at the four relationship "aspects" we have with Him.

Sonship

The first is *sonship*. Sonship is the relationship between a son and a father. Jesus told his disciples they were no longer servants but friends. Servants are rewarded for what they do. Sons and daughters are rewarded for who they are.

My children never did enough chores to earn a nickel. I always wanted them to, but they didn't. But they still got free room, board, rent, and anything else they needed.

My daughter would come to me and say, "Dad, I need four new uniforms, and I want them cute. I want the ones with the colors and stuff."

I would answer, "As old as you are?"

"Yes."

But, you know I would get them for her, because she's mine; she belongs to me. And in like manner, we belong to Christ.

Heir-Ship

After sonship comes *"heir-ship."* Meaning, we understand what we have *in Him*. Romans 8:17 says we're joint heirs with Christ. If we are sons, the Bible says we are also heirs (Gal. 3:29 NKJV). That means we inherit something, so what does that comprise?

The Bible says God has given the earth to Christ as His inheritance (Psalm 2:6–8). Therefore, we share that inheritance with Jesus. "The heavens belong to the Lord, but He has given the earth to all humanity" (Psalm 115:16 NLT).

But the problem with that joint heir-ship is it works both ways. We like that side of it—getting to share in all that Christ has. But it also means that everything you have is His.

That's the part we sometimes cringe at.

Jesus might say to us, "I'd like to use our car to drive across town and pick up old George, and bring him to church."

"*Our* car? Wait a minute, who made the payments on this car, Lord? Who's putting the gas in it?"

"What's yours is mine, and what's mine is yours. And we need some of our money to help build that shelter across the street. I'm going to use some of our time and our strength to minister to someone. I'm going to use our voice to talk to someone about me. I'm going to use our time to go down to the mission and feed those who are hungry and then visit some folks that are sick in the hospital . . ."

So once we understand our sonship, we understand we are also heirs. Once we understand who we are, then we understand what we have.

Discipleship and Throne-Ship

After heir-ship, we move to discipleship. In Christ, we are sons and daughters. What we *possess* is heir-ship. Discipleship is what we must *be* in Christ. We must be under His reign. Under His rule. Under His authority.

The word *disciple* means "a learner." We learn as we receive instruction and guidance from Jesus. Then we do what He says. We are disciples, His followers.

And then, the fourth type of relationship we have with God is "throne-ship." That's what we must *do* in Christ. We must reign with Him presently on the earth and into eternity—whatever He has for us to do.

But some want to jump right to throne-ship without first understanding and honoring sonship, which means building and establishing a relationship with God.

We first need to accept that as God's son or daughter we are in parent-child relationship with Him. And then, as heirs with Christ, we accept that we share in His inheritance with Him and allow Him to use us and all we have for His purposes. And then, as disciples, we continually learn, no matter how old we are in Christ, no matter how long we live. After all that, we can then reign with Him in throne-ship.

Designed to Minister to God

Part of throne-ship is ministry. We are to reign with Jesus as priests (1 Pet. 2:5, 9). We understand that in our ministry as priests, we first are required to minister to Him. Second, we are required to minister to the body of Christ. And third, we are required to minister to the lost. If our priorities get out of order, things get turned around. If we go to the lost first to minister to them, we find that when they come to the church, we can't deliver what we promised.

And so it works like this. You may know these song lyrics: "The praises go up; the blessings come down." That's a truism throughout Scripture. The worship goes up; the heart of God is full. In the law of precipitation, water goes up and creates a cloud. When the cloud is full, what does it do? It pours down rain. Well, as we worship the Lord and honor Him with our lives, we minister to the Lord. The heart of God is full, and He rains down on the church showers of blessings—in the form of gifts and talents and abilities in the church.

Now, with those abilities, we minister to the body of Christ. We make one another strong. We strengthen one another through our gifts and through our talents. We minister to the body so that the body of Christ can become strong.

With a strong body, we minister to the world. When you bring the weight of the world's problems into the church, you must have a strong foundation. Here we are telling people, "God can heal you and deliver you from anything. God can change anything. God can work out anything in your life." But if we bring them into the church and the foundation isn't strong, we hear them say, "I didn't get healed. I didn't get changed. I didn't see any of this power stuff. Someone's preaching. You guys are singing. So what?"

We don't deliver the goods that we promised because the body has not been strengthened. God has given us everything we need through His church. Everything.

Need a miracle? Someone's got the gift of working miracles. You're weak, need faith? Someone's got the gift of faith. Need help financially? Someone's got the gift of giving. Need someone with administrative ability? Someone's got the gift of leading. You need understanding? Someone's got a word of knowledge or wisdom.

The body of Christ, then, should not go out to the world for anything; everything's here in the church. When the body reaches out to the world and brings into the house of God a crack addict, or a person struggling with a broken marriage or homosexuality or severe depression, they can receive help and healing. Right?

And that's the ministry of the priest. Really, all ministering is ministering to the Lord. He said, essentially, "If you give a cup of cold water in my name, whom are you giving it to? You're giving it to me."

So when we minister to the lost, we're ministering to Him. Whose body is it? It's His body.

The First "P" – Person

In order to understand your divine design, you must first understand who you are—how God sees you.

Chapter 2: God Is the One Who Defines Us

"Oh, Lord, I know that the way of man is not in himself. It is not in man who walks to direct his own steps."

This verse at Jeremiah 10:23 (NKJV) shows us how helpless we are apart from God and how desperately we need Him in determining everything in our lives—from His will, to His purpose, to our destiny, to what He has called us to do.

God, when He created us, did not place within us the ability to direct our own path or to understand our way. We are absolutely and completely dependent on God for everything. That was God's design from the beginning. He did not make us as a kind of spiritual toy that He winds up at birth and then just lets go.

We hear people say: "Look deep within you, and you'll be able to straighten your life out" or "I'm going to pull it all together one of these days. I'm going to start doing what I'm supposed to do." But such attitudes are destined to fail—because we are meant to be absolutely dependent upon Him.

I realized this when I first became a Christian. Folks would tease me and say, "Ah, Jesus is just a crutch that you're leaning on." And I thought about that a little bit and said, "No, he's not. He's the whole wheelchair. I can't make it leaning on Him; I've got to be completely carried by Him. Apart from Him, I'm helpless."

Proverbs 3:5–6 tells us to trust in the Lord and not lean on our own understanding. This should be the response to Jeremiah's remark that "the way of man is not within himself and it is not within man who walks to direct his own steps."

Proverbs 3 also says, "In all your ways, acknowledge him, and he shall direct your paths" (NKJV). In all your ways acknowledge Him. At every level, at every strata of life, acknowledge Him.

God Works with Raw Materials

It's important to recognize that it's not the raw material that's important but the development of that raw material. It's not so much the individual, or how many gifts or talents a person may have in his life, but what the development of that life is in the hands of God. Left to ourselves, we don't know where we're going. Searching within ourselves, the way's not there.

You can buy a one-pound bar of iron for five dollars. And you can sell that iron as scrap metal and get five bucks for it. Now, if you take that same iron and melt it down, and you pound it into horseshoes, that same bar of iron now becomes worth five *hundred* dollars. Five hundred dollars for the same bar of iron.

What's the difference? In the blacksmith's hand, it becomes transformed. You take that same bar of iron, melt it down, and make sewing needles out of it, and that bar of iron becomes worth five *thousand* dollars.

Five dollars as a bar of iron. Five hundred dollars as horseshoes. Five thousand dollars as needles.

But you can take that same bar of iron, melt it down, and make tiny springs for fine Swiss watches, and that same bar of iron becomes worth five *hundred thousand* dollars.

So it's not so much the development or what you have; it is how you use it. God's not looking for the most gifted person. God's not looking for the smartest person.

But God is looking for the individual who is available to be molded and shaped by Him.

God jumped over all the Pharisees, all the Sadducees, all the lawyers, all the scribes, all those who were brilliant, to get hold of some dumb fishermen, a slick tax collector, and some other ordinary folks to make and mold into disciples.

It's about Being Available

It's not that He didn't love the Pharisees and the Sadducees—they just weren't available. They had too much going for themselves and trusted in themselves rather than God. So He skipped over them.

Sometimes God doesn't make sense. Why would He choose dumb fishermen who don't know anything to become leaders of the church? Because they were available. As soon as He called Peter, Peter dropped what he was doing. As soon as He called James and John, they dropped their nets. He called Matthew, who immediately left the tax table and followed Jesus.

God looks for people who are available. When it comes to divine design, God created you with a design for your life already in mind. He's not trying to figure out His design for your life, but, rather, it's your job to understand the way that God has made you. We must know, first and foremost, in terms of our person, who we are. Proverbs 20:5 (NKJV) says: "Counsel in the heart of a man is like deep water, but a man of understanding will draw it out." We have the spirit of God flowing within us. We have the presence of God abiding within us. But the wise man of understanding knows how to draw out what God has deposited within him.

Know Him before You Can Know You

Before we can know who we are, we must first understand who He is. Until we know who He is, we will never understand who we are. In John 14:7, we find Jesus saying, "If you had known me, you would have known my Father also; and from now on, you know Him and have seen Him."

Philip, confused, responds with, "Lord, show us the Father and it is sufficient for us." Jesus's answer? "Have I been with you so long, and yet you have not known me, Phillip? He who has seen me has seen the Father. So how can you say, 'Show us the Father'?" (verses 8–9).

Philip had been with Jesus for three years, and yet he didn't know Him.

It never ceases to amaze me how long we can be saved, how long we can be walking with God, how long we can be coming to church and reading the Bible and having morning devotions, and yet, at the same time, not know Him.

Phillip had walked with Jesus. He had talked with Him. He had seen Him perform miracle after miracle after miracle. He had experienced special times with Him. They slept together; they ate together. He witnessed Jesus raise the dead. He heard Him speak prophetically. He understood that "in the beginning was the Word, and the Word was with God, and the Word was God . . . and the Word became flesh" (John 1:1, 14 NKJV).

Phillip had some head knowledge as well as intimate experience, and yet Jesus says, "Have you been with me so long and yet you really don't know me?"

In Matthew 16, verses 13–16, Jesus turns to his disciples and asks, "What are they saying about me? Who do they say I am?"

They answer, "Well, some say that you're John the Baptist, some say Elijah, some say Isaiah, some say one of the prophets."

But then Jesus pushes for more. He's pushing for a clearer understanding. It was important to Jesus that those whom He was walking with and teaching and discipling knew Him and understood who He was.

Jesus then asks Peter: "Who do you say I am?" Peter replies, "You are the Christ, the son of the living God." Jesus then tells him, "Blessed are you, Simon bar Jonah, for flesh and blood has not revealed this to you, but my Father, who is in heaven" (verses 16–17).

Jesus is building His church with a people who know and understand who He is. That's why it's so important to God that you understand and know who He is.

Oh, That We May Know Him

Paul cries out in Philippians 3:10: "Oh, that I might know him." Why would Paul say that? He'd been on three missionary journeys, caught up to the third heaven, and used in miracle after miracle. Jesus even spoke to Paul directly from heaven. And Paul longed to know Him?

Further in the same chapter, Paul says he hopes to forget those things that are behind and press "toward the prize of the mark of the high calling in Christ Jesus" (verse 14 KJV). What is the prize of the high calling in Christ Jesus? It is to know Him. To be intimately acquainted with Him.

God says through David in Psalm 46:10 (NKJV), "Be still and know that I am God." How do we do that? We quit running around, quit running to this meeting and that meeting. Just stop. Be.

First thing: be whoever you are—whatever your problems are, whatever your circumstances are, whatever's going on in your life—just be there. God is saying, "Now while you are where you are, quiet your spirit, quiet your heart. And know that I am God."

That verse is powerful because it is not just a one-time situation. It's not just a one-time act. Time and time again, we are caught up in circumstances and situations and feelings and emotions, and we must learn to accept the place where we are. We can't wish ourselves into other circumstances or wish ourselves away.

You must be who you are. You can't be somebody else. And whoever you are and wherever you are, quiet yourself.

That's why it's so important in the mornings to take some quiet time, to still yourself.

God essentially says to us, "The one thing I want you to understand, in the midst of the storm, in the midst of whatever you're going through, is this: I am God. That means I'm omniscient, all-knowing. I'm omnipotent, all-powerful. I'm omnipresent; I'm everywhere at the same time. Be still and know that I am God."

Psalm 100:3 (KJV) says, "Make a joyful noise unto the Lord. . . . enter into his gates with thanksgiving, and into his courts with praise." In the midst of your praise, in the midst of your worship, while you are in His presence, the psalmist says, "Know that the Lord, he is God. It is he that hath made us."

Over and over again, the Scriptures challenge us to know that He is Lord. Isaiah 60:16 says, "You shall know that I, the Lord, am your Savior." It's so important to know where our help comes from. That we're not going to get it from one place or another; we're going to get it from Him. But before we are confident in that fact, we must know Him.

Constant Pursuit

We need to be in constant pursuit of God. It's almost as if God plays tag with us. He moves on, and we race and race and race to catch Him, and then we catch Him and we finally can say, "Boy, I really know the Lord in this place. I really know Him as Savior. I really know Him as Deliverer." And before we turn around, the Lord has moved on further.

Why does He do this? So we never settle into a complacent satisfaction in our Christian walk. There is always going to be a hunger and thirst to pursue Him. That's what Paul was meant when he said, "Oh, that I might know him." God continues to unfold Himself and blow our minds as He reveals Himself in a greater and a greater way. And the only way we see that unfolding is if we relentlessly pursue Him.

Jeremiah 9:24 (KJV) says, "Let he that glory, glory in this: that he understandeth and knoweth me." Where does our glory come from? From knowing Him.

This Is Eternal Life

In John chapter 17, Jesus wraps up in a nutshell the purpose of His coming, the purpose of the cross, the purpose of eternal life, and the purpose of creation. He says in verse 3: "And this is eternal life: that they may know you." That's why God sent Christ.

That's why Jesus came. That's why God created Adam, then created Eve out of Adam. That's why He raised up a people on the earth. We were created for His good pleasure, but we were created to be in relationship with Him.

This is eternal life—that you may know the only true God and Jesus Christ whom He sent. Our life is wrapped up inextricably with our relationship with Jesus Christ.

So before we can get our lives in gear, we must know Him. Once we know Him, once we are in relationship with Him, once we are intimate with Him, once He is Lord in our lives, then He can define us. He can identify us. He can unfold us.

But first we must trust Him. First we must know Him. First we must recognize that He is God.

God Defines Us

God created me. He deposited gifts in me. Everything I have comes from His hand. I am absolutely, completely dependent upon Him. God answers all those questions the world continues to ask. "Why am I here? What is my purpose? What is life all about?" When we surrender and recognize that He is God, we place ourselves yielded and helpless in His hands, so that He might first begin to identify us and to define us.

It's important to be defined by God. Who are you? What do you say when people ask "Who are you?"

I might say, "Well, I'm Tony Williams."

"No, that's your name. Who are you? What do you say about yourself?"

"I'm a Christian. I'm a born-again believer. I'm—"

"Okay, me too. But who are you?"

It's important that we know who we are. But while it's important that we know who we are, it's equally important that we know who we are not.

When asked who he was, John the Baptist said, "Well, first let me tell you who I'm not. I'm not the Christ."

"Oh, you must be the prophet Elijah."

"No, I'm not."

See, the problem is that people will try to define you. People will put you in a box. People will tell you what your calling is, what you're good at, what you should be doing, what you shouldn't be doing, where you ought to be, what you ought to do. And if you don't have any definition of yourself, you're going to be a composite of what everybody your whole life says about you.

Then, when you try to be what everybody says you should be, you fall flat.

When we don't know who we are, we waste a lot of time trying to be who and what we are not. We need God to come and define us. We need to be pulled aside by God and allow Him to give definition to us, because we waste a lot of time trying to be something we are not, something God never intended us to be. And because of that, many of us waste a lot of years of our lives.

I know, indeed, that I wasted eight years of my life in drug addiction and in jail. I know I was not created to be a prisoner. I was not created to put drugs in my arms. But, somehow, because I didn't know who I was, I was trying to be something that I wasn't, and I wasted a lot of time; I wasted a lot of energy. I caused a lot of heartaches, and I wasted a lot of money.

God never created me to be a drug addict. God never creates anyone to be violated. God never creates anyone to be an alcoholic. God never creates anyone to be an abuser. God never creates anyone to be an outcast.

God had defined John the Baptist, and John knew and understood who he was. When he was asked, "What do you say about yourself?" he answered, "I am the voice of one crying in the wilderness. Make straight the way of the Lord" (John 1:19–23 NKJV). The men sent by the Pharisees asked him, "Why, then, do you baptize, if you are not the Christ or Elijah or the prophet? John answered and said, 'I baptize with water'" (verses 25–26).

John knew what his purpose was. He knew who he was. He said, "There stands one among you whom you do not know. It is he that is coming after me that is preferred before me, whose sandal strap I am not worthy to loose" (verses 26–27). John knew his position, he knew his purpose, and he knew who he was.

See, if you don't let God define you, somebody else will. Others will tell you who you are, what you can do, where you belong, and how far you can go. We buy into that because somebody else has said that, maybe someone in authority. But your definition does not come from any human. Your definition comes from God.

The problem is that we want someone else to punch our ticket. Listen, God is the only one who can punch your ticket. And if God says you're okay, guess what? You're okay. If God says you're in, guess what? You're in. "Let every man be a liar, but let God be true" (Rom. 3:4).

See, Jesus scratched His head on this one in John 5:44 (NIV). He said, "How can you believe since you accept glory from one another but do not seek the glory that comes from the only God?" In other words, "Why are you running around seeking honor and pats on the back from everybody else, and you won't seek a pat on the back from God?"

Jesus, when He taught us to pray, said "Give us this day our daily bread" (Matt. 6:11 NIV). He's saying, "God, give me what I need to make it today. Yesterday's bread is gone. Tomorrow's bread I know will be provided."

It's like the manna God gave to the Israelites in the wilderness. They were instructed not to save any. God provided just what they needed for that day. They rose early, they went out, they got their manna, and they ate it all that day. If they tried to save it, it became infested with worms.

That's why, when we pray, we get our pat on the back from God, so that by the time we get to wherever we're going, we don't need that pat from anyone else. We let God define us.

Jesus taught us to pray, "Give me what I need to make it through today." Bread represents sustenance and all else we need—including the strength we need each day to get through. We pray, "Give me this day my daily bread. Give me the encouragement I need to get through today. No matter what happens or who I run into, or how bad a day I have, I've already had my pat on the back. I've already had my hug this morning from the Lord."

Don't Let Others Put You in Bondage

Peer pressure doesn't stop when you stop being a teenager. We're all pressured.

"What kind of car do you drive? What kind of clothes do you wear? You'd better have the right label on the back of your jeans. Your T-shirt better have the right slogan on it. You'd better have the right tennis shoes on." It varies from culture to culture.

We all want acceptance, yet Jesus says, "Why do you seek that so much from one another and don't seek it from the only one who really counts?" (John 5:44). And that's God.

People respect people who know who they are. Let God define you. Let God give you the understanding. Too often we allow other people or our circumstances to define us, and we end up in bondage to what others think. And in that bondage, we neglect to let God's gift emerge. Because we are afraid of what someone else will say.

Often what we're in bondage to is lies. What other people think and say. What we feel or think about ourselves. And when God says "let every man be a liar," guess what? That includes you and the lies you tell yourself.

When we tell ourselves lies, we're saying God is a liar.

"You don't like me. I've just been terrible, Lord."

"I love you with an everlasting love."

"I can't do that, God."

"You can do all things when I am your strength."

"Yeah, but I'm all alone in this thing. I don't have anyone."

"Didn't I promise that I will never leave you or forsake you?"

"Yeah, but I'm so down."

"I'm the glory and the lifter of your head."

That's why David got in a conversation with himself, and said, "Soul, why art thou cast down? Why don't you hope in God?" (Psalm 43:5 KJV). How do you hope in God? Listen to what God says about you, embrace it, and believe that. That's how David answered his question to himself: "Hope thou in God."

We have pressure inside and outside. Forces and folks trying to define us. Telling us who we are and what we should be doing. And because we are seeking and listening, we are getting our information from someplace other than God. And where we get our information has molded our response to life and who we are.

But God outlines clearly how to fight these pressures intent on molding us. He's given us a suit to put on, that will protect us and arm us.

Chapter 3: God Defines Our Identity

If we don't let God define our identity, our *person*, we run the risk of letting others define us. The way to be sure we are letting God define us is by first putting on the armor of God.

Ephesians the sixth chapter talks about the armor of God. And it's not only for battling the Enemy. It's also good for battling yourself, and the world as well.

> Finally, my brethren, be strong in the Lord and in the power of his might. Put on the whole armour of God that you may be able to stand against the wiles of the devil. For we wrestle not against flesh and blood, but against principalities, against powers, against the rulers of darkness of this world, against spiritual wickedness in high places. Wherefore take unto you the whole armour of God, that ye may be able to withstand in the evil day, and having done all, to stand. Stand therefore, having your loins girt about with truth, and having on the breastplate of righteousness; And your feet shod with the preparation of the gospel of peace; Above all, taking the shield of faith, wherewith ye shall be able to quench all the fiery darts of the wicked. And take the helmet of salvation, and the sword of the Spirit, which is the word of God: Praying always with all prayer and supplication in the Spirit, and watching thereunto with all perseverance and supplication for all saints. (Eph. 6:10–18 KJV)

When we think of the armor of God, the easiest way to memorize it is start at the top and work down.

We first put on the helmet of salvation, and then we get the breastplate of righteousness, then gird our loins with truth, then shod our feet with the gospel of peace.

But let's take a look at the way that it's listed in Scripture, because God always has a purpose in the order in which He presents truth.

What's the first piece of armor? The belt of truth. Second piece of armor? Righteousness. Next? Peace. Then the shield of faith and the helmet of salvation. And then, of course, everything is undergirded with the Word of God and prayer.

Now, let's look at the counterparts of these and see what happens when we buy into what others say—whether it's the enemy of our soul or well-meaning people.

The opposite of truth is a lie. The opposite of righteousness is unrighteousness. The opposite of peace is confusion. The opposite of faith is unbelief. And the opposite of salvation is bondage.

What Happens When We Believe a Lie

Let me show you how this works. If you believe a lie, you're going to do the wrong thing. You'll do the unrighteous thing because you think it's the truth. But then comes confusion—because the outcome doesn't look the way the lie proposed it would. And so you're confused.

"Well, wait a minute," you say. "I thought money was going to make me happy, so I did everything to get money, but I'm confused because it's not making me happy." Or "I thought life was all about sex and seeking pleasure, but that doesn't fulfill me."

In our confusion, we don't know what to believe. We are swimming in unbelief and in bondage to that lie. We believe it when someone tells us we're ugly. When someone tells us we're no good at sports, we're stupid when it comes to school, we'll never make it in that career.

Some people spend their entire life in bondage to lies. They hang on to all kinds of lies, and, to this day, there are certain things they don't do, certain things they don't wear, certain things they don't say, certain things they don't talk about—all because they're in bondage to a lie.

And even though we are saved and we love the Lord, this lie lurks in the back of our hearts and in the back of our minds, and it keeps us from doing what we really believe that God has ordained and purposed and destined for us to do or to be.

We've got fears because of our childhood. Because of things that happened to us when we were younger. We've got stuff that happened to us when we older. We've got things that happened to us yesterday. Things that keep us in bondage to a lie.

Jesus tells us in John 8:32 that "you shall know the truth, and the truth will set you free." So what do we do when we are in bondage to a lie? What do we do when someone else says we can't? What do we do when we the pressure is so great for us not to achieve what we know God has called us to achieve?

What we always do. We go back to the truth. "Let God be true and every man a liar."

"You can't do that!"

"I can do all things through Christ who strengthens me."

"Nobody likes you; nobody cares about you."

"I love you with an everlasting love."

"Listen, you're just by yourself, and who's going to help you? You don't have anybody."

"I will never leave you or forsake you. Lo, I am with you even to the ends of the age."

"You know, you've tried and tried and you keep messing up."

"I am more than a conqueror through Him that loved me."

And so we go back to the truth. "You shall *know* the truth," Jesus says.

Remember the admonition: "Be still and *know* that I am God." It's one thing to *read* the truth; it's another thing to *know* the truth. Jesus says, "I am the way, the truth, and the life" (John 14:6). Once you understand the truth, you begin to do the right thing. When you do the right thing, you have peace in your spirit, peace in your heart, peace in your life. In that peace, your faith is strengthened in Him as a result of knowing the truth. Then that faith leads us to salvation. Salvation from what? Salvation from the bondage and salvation from the lie.

How the Truth Sets Us Free

The writer of Hebrews says, "Come boldly before the throne of grace" (Heb. 4:16). Obtain what you need. Get what you need at the throne of grace. There, "you will know the truth, and the truth will set you free."

This whole process takes place using the sword of the spirit—which is prayer. But it's important that you *allow* the truth to set you free. Free to do what? Free to be. And free to accomplish the purposes of God in your own life.

That is real success. To be who you are. And to accomplish those things that God has given to you to accomplish, thereby glorifying God with your life and living a life of fulfillment.

We can't let peer pressure squeeze us. "Be not conformed," Paul say in Romans 12:2, "to the image of this world." Don't be squeezed into a box. Don't be shaped and formed by outside forces and outside entities. Rather, be *transformed*.

Transformation comes from the inside. It's related to the word *metamorphosis*. When the caterpillar wraps himself in a cocoon, he's a caterpillar. When he comes out of the cocoon, he has been changed completely and absolutely into a beautiful butterfly. No longer is he inching along in a wormlike state. He's floating in the air in a beautiful state.

And so when God says "be transformed by the renewing of your minds"—well, why do we want our minds renewed with the truth? So we now can prove to ourselves this is God's defining—not yours or mine or anyone else's. What does Paul say will be the result? "Then you will be able to test and approve what God's will is—his good, pleasing and perfect will" (NIV).

God called you? Prove it. God asked you to do something? Prove it. It's the will of God that you do something? Prove it. "That you can prove what is the good and acceptable will of God."

Truth will do for you. Truth revealed in His presence. He, Himself, revealed to you through the Word of God. He, Himself, the truth revealed to you in prayer, will do something for you. So if you believed the lie and you did the wrong thing—you're confused, you don't know what to believe, and now you're in bondage to a lie—you always go back to the truth. Because when you go back to the truth, it sets you free.

Sets you free to do what? To do the right thing. To have peace in your spirit, in your heart, about you and God. We are set free from the bondage of the lie we believed. "Know the truth, and the truth will set you free."

Let's take a look at what God's intention was from the very beginning.

> Now the serpent was more cunning than any beast of the field which the Lord God had made. And he said to the woman, "Has God indeed said, 'You shall not eat of every tree of the garden'?" And the woman said to the serpent, "We may eat the fruit of the trees of the garden; but of the fruit of the tree which is in the midst of the garden, God has said, 'You shall not eat it, nor shall you touch it, lest you die.'" Then the serpent said to the woman, "You will not surely die, for God knows that in the day you eat of it, your eyes will be opened, and you will be like God, knowing good and evil."

So when the woman saw that the tree was good for food, that it was pleasant for the eyes, and desirable to make one wise, she took of its fruit and ate. She also gave to her husband with her, and he ate. Then the eyes of both of them were opened, and they knew that they were naked; and they sewed fig leaves together and made themselves coverings.

And they heard the sound of God walking in the garden in the cool of the day, and Adam and his wife hid themselves from the presence of the Lord God among the trees of the garden. Then the Lord God called out to Adam and said to him, "Where are you?"

So he said, "I heard your voice in the garden, and I was afraid because I was naked; and I hid myself." And He said, "Who told you that you were naked? Have you eaten from the tree which I commanded that you should not eat?" Then the man said, "The woman whom you gave me to be with me, she gave me of the tree and I ate." And the Lord God said to the woman, "What is this that you have done?" And the woman said, "The serpent deceived me, and I ate." (Gen. 3:1–13 NKJV)

God Defines Our Identity

God created Adam. And in Adam's perfect creative state, there was no need for faith; there was no need for honesty. He couldn't steal anything because there wasn't anybody to steal from. Didn't have to have faith because God was right there. The only thing that God asked for in the garden was obedience.

Adam was completely and absolutely dependent on God for his identity and for all that he perceived, and all that he understood was to come out of his relationship with God. Adam didn't have anything in him that God didn't put there.

So Adam was created totally dependent on God. Just as we are tied up in our relationship with Jesus.

Adam didn't wake up knowing everything. God communicated everything to him.

"What's that?"

"That's the sun."

"What's that? What's that? What's that?"

But, after the fall, Adam became independent. His identity and his understanding came from outside of God. When God came walking in the cool of the day, Adam was now hidden among the trees, and so God asked Adam a strange question: "Where are you?"

Adam said, "I'm naked. We're hiding because we're naked."

Then God asked him this question: "Who told you that you were naked?" Who provided that information, that you were naked, and then defined nakedness for you? You've always been naked! What do you mean, you're naked? You've been walking around naked all this time, and now all of a sudden someone tells you you're naked? Who told you that?

You see, the problem was that now Adam was getting information and definition from someplace other than God. He was listening to the Devil.

What was the end result of his listening to Satan and his wife instead of God? He got kicked out of the garden. Kicked out of God's presence. Sin entered the world from his act of disobedience to God and his act of obedience to Satan.

Jesus Was Defined by God

Now, when Jesus came, He came as "the second Adam." When He came, He lived a life that was absolutely dependent upon the Father. Jesus as a grown man, thirty-three years old, said (paraphrased), "I only say what Father tells me to say. I only go where Father tells me to go. I only do what Father tells me to do. I don't even come to my own conclusions. I don't even have my own judgments. My judgments are not my own but my Father's. As a matter of fact, I always do those things that please Him" (John 5:19–20).

Today, we would say, "What kind of guy is that? And how old are you? Thirty-three years old? And you can't go anywhere unless your daddy says? You can't do anything unless your daddy says? You don't have enough sense and education to come to your own conclusion? You've got to talk to your daddy?"

And He would say, "Yep."

His brothers came and said, "You know we're going up to Jerusalem to the festival," and He says, "I can't go. Father didn't tell me to go. You guys go on up." And then the next day Jesus goes to the festival because Father said to. He was absolutely governed by the Father.

Why did He go to the pool of Bethesdsa and heal only one man? Because that's what Father told Him to do. Jesus could have had a wife. Jesus could have had kids. Why didn't He? Because Father didn't want it.

Jesus was absolutely, completely, totally dependent upon God for everything.

Remember how the prodigal son wanted to get out of his father's house? He went down into debauchery, but when he finally came to his senses, the Bible says he "came to himself."

In order to come to yourself, you must be what? Beside yourself.

The prodigal son was out of his mind. When he finally came to himself, he said, "I'm going back to Father. I'd rather be a servant in Father's house than Mr. Big-Shot out here." And so he goes back to his father.

Whenever we come to our senses, we go back to Father's house. Once in Father's house, we're under the rule and reign of Father.

We're absolutely dependent upon Him.

Trials do not come to make us strong. Trials come to show us how weak we are and how much we need God. My trials make me run into the arms of God, and then I can be strong in Him and in the power of His might. They don't come to make me strongly and fiercely independent.

What we are strong in rivals God. What we are weak in becomes usable in service to God.

Dependency Equates with Power

When we are strong in something, we say, "God, I got it." And we just go on to do certain things without prayerfully considering them. Jesus was absolutely dependent upon the Father for everything, and though He was the most dependent man that ever lived on the face of the earth, He was the most powerful man that ever lived.

Dependency on God equates with power. Independence from God equates to weakness and disaster. It's so important that we recognize that.

When we are dependent upon God to identify us, we reject any other definitions. People called Jesus all sorts of things, but He knew His true identity. He let God define Him.

Satan doesn't care if you believe in God. He doesn't care if you go to church. He doesn't care if you go buy the best Bible or hang around with other Christians. But what he does care about is your relationship with God. He wants you to have no relationship with Him.

Why is it, when it's time to interact with God, time to pray, you get sleepy? Why is it, when it's time to read the Word, you get tired? Why is it, when it's time for you to develop and build your relationship, that's when Satan fights? If he can get us so busy at the church, we'll miss our calling.

Remember what our calling is? Into His presence. He says, in essence, "I called you to be with me. I'll send you to do some things, but when you get done, I want you to be with me."

The Enemy will get us so busy doing stuff that we'll get burned out, frustrated at everything else. He doesn't want you to have a relationship with God because he knows that if you do, God is going to define you.

And when God does that, you're going to understand who you are, you're going to understand your authority as a believer, and you're going to understand your purpose and what God designed and desires for you to do so you can accomplish the purpose of God. That's what he is fighting.

Satan cannot stop you from believing in God. That's not his objective. He just doesn't want you to have a relationship with Him.

Chapter 4: Relationship Is the Key to Our Identity

Jesus said, "Have you been with me so long and you don't know me? You don't know who I am? I'm God." Relationship with Him is the key to our identity. Because out of that relationship comes our definition. Jesus knew who He was, and He wanted everyone else to know who He was. He understood His purpose, and He fulfilled it all. Isn't that amazing, that He could do what we can't seem to accomplish? See, it was all due to His relationship with His Father.

In the New Testament, the Father never called Jesus anything except "Son." He never said, "He's the bright and morning star, He's the wheel in the middle of the wheel, He's the lily of the valley, He's the savior of your soul, He is the master of mankind, He is the ruler, He is Christ the king." Every time He addresses Jesus, He says, "That's my son."

See, when you want to emphasize relationship and closeness, you say, "This is my husband." You don't say, "Oh, this is James." And when referring to your children, you say, "This is my son. This is my daughter Megan. This is my daughter Charity. This is my son Tony Junior."

And so, when God speaks from heaven at the baptism of Jesus and says, "That's my son. That's my boy," He's speaking and pointing to their relationship. And Jesus always referred to God as His Father. "I'm going to Father's house." Jesus taught His followers, "When you pray, say 'our Father.'" Our Father. Because He is pointing to the relationship. That is what is most important to Him.

By our relationship with God we are defined. We understand who He is, and we understand who we are. Galatians 4:4–7 says: "But when the fullness of the time had come, God sent forth His son, born of a woman, born under the law, to redeem those who were under the law, that we might receive the adoption of sons. And because you are sons, God sent forth the spirit of His Son into your hearts, crying out 'Abba, Father!' Therefore you are no longer a slave, but a son. And if a son, then an heir of God through Christ" (NKJV).

Remember, servants are rewarded for what they do. Sons are rewarded for who they are. That's why, when Jesus taught us to pray, He was basically saying, "When you come to pray, say 'Hey, Dad!'" We don't reward our children for what they do. Lord knows if we did, they would be homeless and hungry, eating at the soup kitchen.

If I had to equate what I give my children to the work they do, it would be over. They would be in trouble. They get whatever they need because they belong to me. They are mine, so I'll do what it takes to provide for them.

We must understand that relationship with God is valued *by worship* and not by works. That our identity is tied up in our relationship, not tied up in the rules. Sure, works are important. What we do is important. Ephesians 2:10 tells us that we were created in Christ Jesus for the purpose of good works. James tells us that without works, faith is dead. Titus 3:8 says that we should be careful to maintain good works.

But good works are an outgrowth, not the source, of our identity.

So when I come to prayer, it's not based on "Okay, I went to church every week. I haven't missed one day in a year. I went to Bible study. I've been getting up and having my devotions. I've been reading the Bible every day. I haven't cussed at anybody in a year. I've been trying to be nice to my brother and even lent my sister a few dollars. I called my mother last month. I make sure on Sunday that I talk to her, and I respect everybody. So therefore, God, you have to do this for me."

Many don't pray because they think their worth in coming to Him is based on works, on obeying and keeping all the rules, when, in reality, it is based on their relationship with God. We're to come as we are, and if there is correcting to be done, we can trust that Father's going to correct us and get us right.

How do you think most people would answer if you asked, "What does it mean to be a Christian?" They'd say, "Oh, you got to come to church. Got to read your Bible every day. And you got to do this, and you got to do that. Keep the Ten Commandments, honor your father and mother, do what your pastor says . . ."

None of that means being a Christian. Then what does? Being born again by the spirit of God and being in a relationship with God the Father as a son or daughter. That's what it means to be a Christian.

We have all these preconceived notions and ideas. Listen, the rules are important. Jesus said, "If you love me, keep my commandments." But the rules are important for living—not so much for life. Jesus didn't say, "This is eternal life, that you keep all the rules." No. He said, "This is eternal life, that you *know God*."

That's where your life springs from and what governs you as you live. Yes, there are rules, guidelines, commandments. But don't let those things identify you. That's Old Testament. Your identity comes with Calvary's cross. Your identity comes through the death, burial, and resurrection of Jesus Christ. Your identity is wrapped up completely and totally in your relationship with Jesus Christ. Your approach to God is based on the finished work of Calvary. Not on anything else.

When we understand our identity is defined by relationship and not by rules, it brings us into a much greater understanding when we approach God as our father. We approach Him out of our relationship because of who we are and who He made us to be. He sent the spirit of His Son into our hearts, the spirit of adoption whereby we cry "Abba, Father."

There are several ways to get into a family. You can marry into one. Well, we are the bride of Christ. You can be born into a family.

Well, we have been born again. Or you can be adopted into a family. We've been adopted into God's family.

Abba is an affectionate word like Dada or Daddy. Instead of saying "Daddy," you say "Abba." And so when he says that the spirit of adoption comes in and we cry "Abba, Father," that means we have full understanding of our relationship with God. We know that it is based on love and what He has done. We also know who we are, because we call Him Father. We recognize His authority to define us.

We're All on Level Ground

In the world, what you have plus what you do *equals* who you are. That's the formula for identity in the world. You got a lot of money? You're someone. What do you do for a living? Oh, you're a doctor or a lawyer? You're valuable. You're just a street sweeper? Well, you're a nobody.

However, in the kingdom, who you are equals what you have and what you do. Because I am God's son, I live this way. Because I am His son, I honor Him with my life. Because I am His son, I have all things.

Who you are equals what you have. It's important that we know that. Otherwise, we will always be caught up in the church with what we have and what we do. "I'm the pastor, so that makes me above everyone."

That's not so. We are all His.

There's no big I's and little yous; there are no levels here. In terms of our relationship with God, we are all on level ground.

So don't let what you have and what you don't have and what you do and what you can't do equal who you are. That's the way the world wants to define you.

Say, "I belong to Him. God has defined me." That equates to what you have. And what else do you have? "I have all things in Him. I can do all things through Christ who strengthens me." That is the equation we use to define our life and our understanding of who we are.

Jesus Knew Who He Was

Jesus knew who He was. And because Jesus knew who He was, He had no problem *being* who He was. In John 8:14, Jesus says, "Even if I bear witness of myself, my witness is true."

Listen to what else He says: "I know where I came from and where I am going. You do not know where you came from or where you are going." Jesus says, "I came from God; I'm going to God."

John 13:3 says, "Jesus, knowing that the father had given all things into his hands and that he had come from God and was going to God, rose from supper, laid aside his garments, took a towel, girded himself, poured water into a basin, and began to wash the disciples' feet and wipe them with the towel with which he was girded."

Listen, when you know who you are, there is no job too small. There are no menial tasks. There is nothing that is "beneath you" in the kingdom.

When you know who you are, you recognize that there is no one who is better than you in God's sight, so you don't have to feel intimidated by anyone. But you also understand that you are not better than anyone else.

So we treat each person with dignity and with respect. Jesus, knowing that God put all things in His hands, knowing where He came from, knowing where He was going, took a towel and girded Himself.

I can go to the rescue mission in the morning; I can work with alcoholics and drunks; I can tell them about Jesus; I can wash them up, get them dressed, feed them, and serve tables.

Then, in the afternoon, I can go sit at the mayor's office and share my opinion about the city's needs and not be intimidated.

It's not beneath me to help someone on the street and then in the afternoon go talk to the mayor and share with her what's on my heart, the issues I am addressing.

Yes, people have positions; we're not talking about that. We're talking about who you are—your identity. When you know who you are, you can sweep the bathroom, clean the toilet, wipe the mirrors, and then make your way to the pulpit and preach.

Here Jesus was—the Creator of the world, about to go to sit at the right hand of the Majesty on High as the King of Kings, Lord of Lords—with a towel around Him, kneeling and washing some dirty feet. But because He knew who He was, washing feet was no big deal.

When you know who you are, no one can bump you around. No one can elevate you; no one can throw you down. God says to us, "You were bought with a price. You are my son; you are my daughter. That's never going to change, and I love you." When we understand that relationship, prayer is so much more enjoyable and wonderful. Instead of a chore that we do, it's a relationship we have.

Jesus knew who He was naturally and spiritually. He knew His natural heritage–that He was the son of Mary, who was a descendant of King David. He knew what tribe He was from through His stepfather Joseph—the tribe of Judah. He understood that He was a Jew. He knew where He came from. But He also knew who He was spiritually.

Paul knew who he was. He knew that he was of the tribe of Benjamin. He knew that he was a Pharisee of Pharisees. He knew that he was a Jew. He knew all those things naturally, but he also knew spiritually who he was.

If you don't like me, hey, talk to God. Because I am whatever He made me. He identified me, and I want to be a vessel of honor. I want to be an instrument that He can use.

It's part of my design. It's my makeup. It's who I am. I can't cry about the family I was born into. I don't complain about the color of my skin. I'm not angry because I'm not on this side of the tracks or that side of the tracks. I can't be angry because my parents couldn't afford to send me to college. Or that someone else was born with a silver spoon in his mouth.

The sooner I can get defined by God, the sooner I can get on with being who He created me to be.

Avoid the Identity Traps

When we don't allow God to define us in that manner and in that way, we end up in ruts and in traps in our lives. A trap has a purpose; a snare has a purpose. They're devices for catching and holding you. Holding you back from being what God designed and purposed for you.

The one thing that you have to recognize about a trap is that it is stronger than you. But thank God for the promise in Psalm 91—that He'll deliver you from anything that is keeping you from being and doing what God created you to be and to do. That is one thing that we must have absolute confidence in—that nothing can change the determined will of God for your life. So, we pray, "God, first identify me and tell me who I am. Then, Lord, set me free from any traps. And give me purpose to fulfill your will."

This reminds me of a story about an old preacher who was in the back of the church emptying the trash. Down the back alley of the church comes a little kid carrying a rusty old cage filled with birds.

The preacher says, "What do you have in that cage?"

The boy says, "Uh, just some old birds. I caught them over there in the field."

And the preacher says, "What are you going to do with those birds?"

"Oh, I'm going to take them back to the house, poke a stick at them for a while."

Preacher says, "Oh, and then what are you going to do?"

"Well, I'll pull me out a few feathers, make me an Indian cap. Make my friends some Indian caps and stuff."

He says, "Well. Then what are you going to do?"

He says, "I got an old cat. I'll throw the birds out and let the cat have them."

The old preacher says, "Son, how much you want for those birds?"

He answers, "Sir, you don't want these birds. They don't have any color to them; they're just some old brown field birds."

"How much?"

"You don't want these birds. They can't sing. They're not good for food. They're not good for pets. They're really useless. They're just some old field birds."

He says, "Son, how much do you want for them?"

The boy sees a chance to make a profit, so he says, "Give me two dollars, Preacher."

So the preacher reaches in his old baggy pants and pulls out two bucks and gives them to the boy. The boy hands him the old rusty cage that the birds are in. Then the boy walks down the alley, stops, and turns around to see what the preacher is going to do with the birds.

The preacher opens the cage and shakes it. Lets the birds out.

Here's another story. One day Jesus is in the back streets of life. He sees Satan coming down the alley with a cage full of folks.

Jesus says, "What do you have there, Satan?"

He says, "Uh, just some old folks. People."

"What are you going to do with them?"

"I'm going to poke at them for a while."

"Then what are you going to do?"

"I'm going to tear their limbs off one by one."

"Then what?"

"Cast them into hell."

Jesus said, "How much for those folks?"

Satan said, "You don't want these guys. There're no kings or princes in here. There are no recording artists here. There're no great preachers that have preached around the world in here. There are no guys with special talents or rich people that have a lot of money."

Jesus asks, "How much for them?"

Satan sees a chance to make a profit, so he says, "I'll take your life."

And Jesus says, "You got it."

Every week some pastor is shaking the cage from the pulpit. Letting you know that the price has been paid and you are free to be exactly who He created you to be. Not a parrot. Not a robin. Just whoever you are. But you have to come out of the cage. Take God at His word, thank Him for who He made you and for whatever gifts He has deposited in your life, and fly off to do the will of God for the glory of God.

God promises that He will deliver us from any snare, any trap, that is hindering us and holding us back from becoming everything He created and purposed us to be. But first we must know who He is beyond a shadow of a doubt. We must be convinced.

Dr. Tony Williams

The Second "P" – Position

We must position ourselves so that God can do exactly what He has purposed and designed to do in our lives.

Chapter 5: Know Your Place

We looked at the first P in our divine design: Person. Our identity. Who we are. There is a great need for us to know and understand exactly who we are. When we don't know who we are, life becomes very frustrating and full of disappointment because we don't see ourselves as God sees us. Oftentimes we live as others see us. But the only way to live a life that is full and fulfilling is to live as God sees us.

Once we understand *who* we are, then we must position ourselves.

Positioning Ourselves in Line with Divine Design

To be in position means to be in the right place. It means to have the right attitude. It means to see things from the right point of view. If we don't position ourselves and we end up in the wrong place, oftentimes we will be looking at things from the wrong point of view.

Our place is our location in relationship to everything else. And it particularly concerns our heart. Of all the things in our lives, we must get our hearts in position, and we must be brutally honest about where we are.

Position is so important. Ask anyone who plays sports. If a quarterback gets out of position or a fullback or a tackle falls out of position in football, the team will lose the game.

A boxer always has to take the right position in order to defend himself and throw the best punches. So, too, we must be positioned right. We must be in the right place. The right situation. The right standing.

There Are No Accidents When We're in Position

God assigns each person an appointed time and place. When we understand our place and who we are, and we get an understanding of who He is, we recognize that there are no accidents. There are no coincidences. God is never wringing His hands, never sweating it out, never scratching His head about the next thing to do. There is just His design.

You don't see any "Oops, the sun forgot to come up" or "Oops, the earth forgot to rotate on its axis," or "Oops, winter lost its place and didn't show up." There is a design to everything that God has made. And He has promised that He will meet us where we are and position us where He designed us to be if we are out of place.

What's our place? It's the area that is occupied by our purpose and by our person.

In Genesis 2:4–5 (NKJV), after we're given the story of creation and God has rested on the seventh day, it says, "This is the history of the heavens and the earth, when they were created, in the day that the Lord God made the earth and the heavens, before any plant of the field was in the earth, before any herb of the field had grown. For the Lord God had not caused it to rain."

Rain is symbolic in Scripture of blessings, of the presence of God. Rain pours down from Him. But rain can also mean trouble. Jesus spoke about a wise man who built his house on sand, and the winds and the storms came to undermine it (Matt. 7:24–27). Sometimes blessings will blow away our house quicker than a storm or trouble because we cannot handle the blessings of God, or we cannot handle increase in our life.

We need water in order to survive. We need water for growth. Often, in our own lives and in our own circumstances, until God gets us in place, He will cause it not to rain in our situation—to shower down blessings. He will not rain in our lives until He gets us in position.

Think about how we look for a mate. It's got to be the right person. It's got to be the right time, and it's got to be in the right place. Sometimes you've got the right person, but it's not the right time. Sometimes, it's the right time and the right place, but it's the wrong person. When all three of those factors come together, it makes for a marvelous relationship that can last a lifetime.

And so it is in God's dealing with our life. He wants the right person—you. So you've got to know who you are and appreciate that this is the way God made you. Got the right person, now you have to get in the right place, and then, at the right time, God will do what He desires to do. He will not act before the time is right.

When He had Adam in place, He planted the garden and then He placed Adam where He wanted him. Because of sin and disobedience, Adam moved himself out of the right place. And though Adam still was the right person, he was moved from the right place, and so life went on and he passed sin down from generation to generation until now.

Wandering Lost

This is why it is so important that we get placed by God. That's not always about geographic location. It's the place you are in terms of your relationship with God and your understanding of who He is and who He desires to be in your life.

First Corinthians, the twelfth chapter, talks about God setting up the church. It says in verse 18, "But now God has set the members, each one of them, in the body, just as it pleased him."

He didn't set them according to what each wanted to do. The Bible says that when we are set in the body of Christ by God, we are to be content with our position, fulfilled as we are giving God the greatest glory that we can with our lives.

But note, the Scripture says, "God has set members in the body just as it pleased him."

Remember, Jesus said, "I always do those things that please him." Jesus was always in the right place at the right time, and He was always the right person. You never see Jesus out of breath, do you? You never see Him running anywhere; you never see Him missing anything. He waited before He went up to Bethany to deal with Lazarus. He's always in the right place. And, too, God has set the members, each one of us, in the body just as it pleases Him. If that's so, then it's important that we understand the place He's set for us.

Proverbs 27:8 gives us a hint. "Like a bird that wanders from his nest, is a man who wanders from his place" (NKJV). There is a sense of feeling lost when we are out of place, and no one else can understand it. We can't really explain it, but we're just kind of uncomfortable.

Have you ever been there? You're saved; you love the Lord; you are filled with the spirit of God. But there is an uneasiness or a sense of wandering. Just as in the parable of the prodigal son, the pitiful older son is in the house but doesn't have a clue what's going on. He's in the house, but he's lost. Compare this to Jesus Christ, who is always in communication with the Father. He is always in the right place, and His desire is to always be with Father. And He talks incessantly about Father's house.

Psalm 14:1 says, "The fool has said in his heart, there is no God." What is a more dangerous position to be in? Lost outside the house, where you can recognize your need of salvation and come back in, or lost *in* the house, where you think everything's okay and just dandy, and you just go along ignorant of your lack of position? That was the problem with the Pharisees and the Sadducees.

So the pitiful son is in the house, doesn't know what's going on, comes in out of the field, and asks the servants, "What's going on?" Here he comes to his own house and has to ask the servants who work there what the commotion is. And when he finds out what is going on, he gets all upset. Folds his arms and pouts.

And the father goes over and asks him, "What's wrong?"

The son tells him, "I did everything you said. I've been going to church, I've been doing everything—"

"You've been lost in the house—"

"But I've been doing everything I'm supposed to do religiously."

But he didn't have a relationship with his father.

He complains, "You never killed the fatted calf for me."

The father turns to him and says, "All that is mine is yours. All you had to do was ask."

The son wouldn't come in the house. Kind of like a four-year-old who has to go to a party, and there are only girls there. He's sitting in the corner and looking around, and the girls all have these fluffy dresses on, and they're all laughing and giggling at him, and he feels like a dork.

"I don't want to be here. I want to be playing baseball with my buddies," he complains. But then the party goes on, and the girls start having fun. They are playing games, and the ice cream comes out, the cake is delicious, everything is great. But he is still mad and thinks, "I'm not going to have fun at this party."

Some of us were just like that as kids. We sat there and kept our arms folded and watched the party from a distance. We could have had a great time, but we decided we didn't want to be there.

That's how it was with the pitiful son. You can be in the body of Christ—in the house—but still be out of position.

Think about the proverb about the bird wandering from its nest. When birds wander from their nest, they are tired. They've been flying awhile. They want to go back to their warm bed, but they are exhausted and frustrated because they can't find it; they have wandered away.

So is a man who wanders away from his place. He is frustrated and exhausted, and he needs to get back to where he belongs.

Others Who Wandered Lost

In Genesis the third chapter, God asks Adam a probing question: "Adam, where are you?" Now, here's an omniscient God who knows everything asking, "Adam, where are you?" He was not trying to locate him geographically; He wanted Adam to identify his own position. Adam said, "I was afraid, because I was naked, so I hid myself." He had the wrong information and was getting his information from the wrong place.

But God wanted Adam to understand where he himself was. God is always seeking you, whatever place you are in. Even when you are out of place, He is seeking you to bring you back into place. And He then gave a prophetic word to Adam, to indicate that mankind would one day be back in place. The serpent would bruise the heel of the promised deliverer, but that deliverer would bruise the serpent's head. That was a prophetic utterance about the coming of the Lord Jesus, stated to make clear we would be one day be put back in place.

Much like Adam, Elijah had gotten out of place (1 Kings 18 and 19). He had run from Jezebel after his great victory, where he had called down fire from heaven on those worshipping Baal, and Jezebel announces, "This day I am putting a hit out on Elijah." So what does he do? He takes off running. He runs and runs and runs, and he asks God to kill him. Well, if he wanted to die, why didn't he just let Jezebel do it?

Elijah finds a cave. Like Adam, he is hiding. But it says in chapter 19 verse 9, "And he went into the cave and he spent the night in that place." Not the place God wanted him in, but he was in that place. "And behold, the word of the Lord came to him and said to him, 'What are you doing here, Elijah?'"

Has God ever asked you that? "What are you doing here in depression? What are you doing here doubting? What are you doing here as frustrated as you are? What are you doing here as lonely as you are? What are you doing here?" God not only wants us to recognize that we are sometimes in hiding and out of place, He wants us to think about what are we doing there. Sometimes our place can be the condition of our heart and the spiritual condition of where we may find ourselves. God wants us to understand exactly where that is, and He wants us to understand how we got there. He asks us, "What are you doing here?" We never have the right answer.

Elijah tells God, "I . . . I . . . uh. I did everything you told me to do, and I'm the only one left in all the world."

God says, "Listen, I have seven thousand left that haven't bowed their knee to Baal. You're 7,001."

But Elijah replies, "I'm all alone, and my enemy is seeking to kill me."

You ever had a pity party? I must have had a million of them. "Oh, God, I'm trying to do the best I can, and people don't like me and I don't like them. I prayed and I fasted and I did everything you told me to do, and look at me!"

God says, "What are you doing throwing a pity party? You don't belong there!"

If we stop to explain, our answers really won't make sense.

In Elijah's case, God tells him to go out and stand on the mountain, so Elijah stands on the mountain.

The Still, Small Voice

Can't you picture that old prophet? I see Elijah with a great long white beard, long hair, a rugged, weatherworn face, and a great big mantle that's blowing in the wind. And God sends a strong wind, and this wind is blowing, and Elijah's mantle is flying back, and he stands in the face of that wind. But God's not in the wind.

So then God sends an earthquake, and the earth trembles beneath his feet, and the old prophet gets his bearing and stands and digs in. But God's not in the earthquake.

He sends a consuming fire, and Elijah doesn't flinch. But God's not in the fire. He's not in the things around him, not anywhere.

Then God speaks in a still, small voice. And when He does it, this great prophet falls, wraps his mantle around his face, and begins to tremble. And then the voice says, again, "What are you doing here?" A still, small, voice that Elijah hears in his heart.

God speaks strongest and clearest when He speaks to our heart. We are not given signs and wonders to receive our communication from God. In the still, small voice, He speaks to Elijah and instructs him, and Elijah rises and goes and anoints Elisha.

"What are you doing here? You're out of your place." And God sends him to the right place, after putting Elijah in the right position.

A Time to Leave and Find Your Place

Let me give you a couple of examples of why place is so important. One is found in Genesis 13. God comes to Abraham (verse 14) and says, "Lift up your eyes now and look from the place where you are. Northward, southward, eastward, and westward. For all this land I will give to you and your descendants forever. Look now, from the place you are in." Here we see God putting Abraham in position.

In Genesis 30:25, we see Jacob has been tricked by Laban. He's in that place because he fled from his father's house. But in time, he knew he had to leave to be in the right position with God. "And it came to pass, when Rachel had born Joseph that Jacob said to Laban, 'Send me away, that I may go to my own place and to my country.'"

When we are babes in Christ, we don't have a clue where our place is. But there comes a time when He wants us no longer to be babes but to rise and journey to our own place. Don't you wish that happened in real life? That when your kids had grown and matured, they would go find their own place? That's what we are designed to do. But some kids do what? They're forty-five and still at home. "Mom, what's for dinner?"

The plan is you raise them until they're mature, teach them what they need to learn in order to stand on their own, then, when they come of age, they go out and find their own place. To the place that God has purposed and designed for them.

That's the responsibility of the church—to prepare new believers so that they can rise up and take their place. Some they send out to begin new ministries; some remain where they are and find their place in their home church.

Jacob says, "Listen, it's time for me to go to my own place." And when he got to his own place, God blessed him richly, and Israel began to flourish.

What was Laban's response when Jacob told him he was leaving? Jacob was heading off with his sons and all that God had blessed him with, and the Bible says, "Early in the morning Laban arose, and kissed his sons and daughters and blessed them. Then Laban departed and returned to his place" (Gen. 31:55 NKJV).

There are times when you, in ministry and in leadership, will help someone find their place, but then your responsibility is to return to your place.

God speaks to the Israelites in Exodus 23:20 (NKJV): "Behold, I send an Angel before you to keep you in the way, and to bring you into the place which I have prepared." The place that you are to be is the place that God has prepared for you. Remember what Jesus says? "I go to prepare for you." Prepare what? A place. There is another place that we are all going to, where we will spend eternity, but there is also a place here.

In Exodus 33:21, The Lord speaks to Moses and says, "There is a place by me, and you shall stand on the rock." God positions Moses on the rock; He puts him in a place of authority.

And as we submit to God, where is our place? We are seated in heavenly places in Christ Jesus (Eph. 2:6–7).

God has a place for you. It will not be crowded in heaven. Everyone will have their place, and everyone will be happy with their place, and everyone will be right next to Jesus.

When We're out of Place, We Can't Hear God's Voice

When young Samuel was sent to serve in the temple, the voice of the Lord came to him one night and said, "Samuel. Samuel." And Samuel answered, "Speak, Lord; for thy servant heareth" (1 Sam. 3:10 KJV). So when we are in place, we will hear the voice of God. Don't you ever doubt it. He doesn't just speak to the big guys and the prophets and those you see in national ministry. He spoke to young Samuel, and He will speak to you as well, when you are in place.

Our ultimate place is to be with Him. But in our lives, we have a little trouble sometimes. Consider Jesus's disciples. After Jesus died, they are at the Sea of Tiberias, seven of them, and Peter says "I'm going fishing." Now, what did Jesus tell him? "I'll make you fishers of men" (Matt. 4:19).

But Peter says, "I'm going fishing." In other words, "Jesus is gone. I can't see Him, can't feel Him, can't touch Him, so I'm going back to what I know best." And the rest of them say, "Hey, we're going with you." So they get into the boat, and that night they catch no fish. Not a one.

There are times in our lives when we are fishing everywhere, rowing everywhere, trying to get something, and we have nothing to show for it because we are out of place, putting ourselves where *we* want to be and going after what *we* thought we needed.

Peter probably said, "Well, I have to make a living, and I make my living fishing. Jesus isn't here anymore. I could deal with it while He was here, whipping up those miracles of fish and loaves and stuff, but He's not here now."

What happened next? "When the morning came, Jesus stood on the shore, but the disciples did not know it was Jesus."

When we are out of place, we miss God. Jesus comes, trying to speak to us, and we're missing Him because we're not in the right place in our heart to hear Him.

Then Jesus asks the disciples a question. "Children, have you any food?" (John 21:5 NKJV). What he's really asking is, do you have anything at all to show for doing it your way? The answer comes back, "No. We don't have anything to show for all our hard effort."

So Jesus tells them, "Cast the net on the right side of the boat, and you will find some." So they cast, and now they are not able to draw the net in because of the multitude of fish (verse 6). There's a dynamic truth here. They did exactly what He said to do. "Therefore, that disciple whom Jesus loved said to Peter, 'It's the Lord!' Now when Simon Peter heard that it was the Lord, he put on his outer garment (for he had removed it), and he plunged into the sea" (verse 7). Problem was, they didn't recognize Jesus. They were out of place. Then, when they did what Jesus said, they suddenly recognized Him.

Jesus is made real in our obedience. He is made real through our obedience. He says in John 14:21 (NKJV), "He who has my commandments and keeps them, it is he who loves me." And so Peter swims to shore. We don't know what he and Jesus talked about all the time that he was on shore, but he got some private time while the others were out in the boat dealing with the fish they'd caught.

Sometimes it's good to jump out of the boat. Someone will say, "Just stick with the boat. We'll get there; can't you see that we're headed to shore?" But some people will jump out of the boat, saying, "Listen, I want something more than that, and I need it now."

Peter made a beeline for Jesus. When the others got to the shore, they dragged up the fish they had caught, but here is the thing that blows my mind. In verse 9 it says, "As soon as they had come to land, they saw a fire of coals there, and fish laid on it, and bread."

Hmmm. Jesus told them to bring the fish they'd caught. After fishing and sweating all night and catching nothing, they did what Jesus said. But even when they finally got to shore, Jesus already had what they were looking for, and He had it cooked with some bread on the side.

Just as with Elijah, God was saying to the disciples, "What are you doing there? I've got everything you need. You want fish? I have fish! You want them cleaned and cooked? They're cleaned and cooked."

He says, "Listen, you don't have to do a thing. Come and dine. I had what you needed all along. And here you are fishing all night, sweating, troubled. All night and day, you're worn out and don't have anything to show for it. If you had come to me, I had exactly what you needed. And not only that, it's cooked, ready to eat, and here's bread to go with it."

Be Honest about the Place You're In

So they eat. And when they're finished, Jesus turns to Peter and says, "Hey, Peter, do you love me?"

Now, that's kind of embarrassing, putting Peter on the spot in front of his friends. But Peter answers, "Yes, Lord."

"Okay, then do what I tell you to do. Feed my sheep. Okay? Listen, do you love me?"

"Yes."

"Then do what I tell you to do. Feed my sheep."

The third time, Jesus asks, "Peter, do you love me?" Peter says, "Lord, you know that I love you." Jesus pushed Peter to look at his response, to see the place he was in before his Lord (John 21:15–17, paraphrased).

We need to be honest with God. "God, I'm afraid. This morning, to tell the truth, I'm over here in a place of discouragement. Could you please come and get me? Because I can't seem to get out by myself. Would you lift me and carry me over there to encouragement? I know I shouldn't be here. I don't know how I got here. I let things get to me, but here I am nevertheless."

Maybe you need to say, "Could you meet me over here in anger? Because I am really mad!" What good does it do to say you are not mad when you are really mad? Especially when you are talking to the Lord? "I am angry. And I shouldn't be angry with that person. God, forgive me, but, Lord, I am really angry. Would you meet me here in my anger and help me out of here, because it's got me trapped? I can't seem to shake it myself."

He will meet us. His desire is to meet us where we are with the purpose of taking us where He has designed and purposed us to be. Our place and position.

Our position was lost. Jesus came into our lost-ness. Our position was sin. Jesus came into our sin. He became sin for us, to take us to the place that God had designed for us from the very beginning, and that is in fellowship with the Father.

One Step at a Time

First, we need to know who God is. That's all-consuming important because that means that we will trust Him. Then we trust Him to identify us. Then we allow Him to help us locate ourselves so that we honestly know where we are, so that we can start moving to where we are supposed to be. With His guidance, with His strength, with His help, and by His power.

I have a saying that I like: Life is hard by the yard, but it's a cinch by the inch. Don't try to become an overnight wonder or an overnight spiritual giant. Let God meet you where you are and know the ground that you covered so that you don't have to cover it again.

When you go in great leaps, you don't have any understanding of what ground you've covered. When you move forward inch by inch, you see and understand the ground beneath you, and you are solidly and firmly in Christ.

When I fall, I ask God one question: "Why do you have me flat on my back, Lord? Why am I on my face? You must have put me here to tell me something. I'm listening. Speak to my heart."

When you fall, ask God, "What do you want? Speak to me. Do you want me to change something? Speak to my heart. You have my undivided attention. I am laid out before you."

"Where are you?" God asks.

Just tell Him. He will be glad to meet you there. He met Elijah at the cave; He met Adam in the garden, where he was hiding behind the fig leaves. He will meet you right where you are, and He will take you where He wants you to be.

Dr. Tony Williams

The Third "P" – Purpose

Our purpose is our destiny, our calling. What God has gifted us to do. And discovering and fulfilling that purpose is the key to success and fulfillment in our life.

Chapter 6: Letting God Define Our Purpose

We first must understand who we are, and once we do, we next must understand our place, or our position in God. Then, the next step is to understand our purpose.

Your purpose is your destiny. Your purpose is your reason for living. Your purpose is the goal for which you are striving. Your purpose is your course.

The apostle Paul said, "I finished my course." He fulfilled his purpose on earth. But he couldn't have made that claim if he hadn't first understood his relationship to Christ and the position God had placed him in.

Purpose is an objective that you are working toward attaining. Our life and our perspective in life change when we catch a glimpse of God's purpose for us. When we understand our purpose, our whole value system changes.

When we understand our purpose, we change ladders, so to speak. When you are climbing the ladder of the world, what's at the top? Fame, money, power, possessions, recognition—all those things. We strive to get to the top of that ladder.

What's at the bottom of the ladder of the world? Stuff like forgiveness, meekness, faith, love, sacrifice, humility, honesty. The ladder of the world expects you to step on whoever you must to get to the top, to reach the fame and fortune awaiting you.

The ladder that reaches the kingdom of God, however, is the reverse. Those things at the top of the world's ladder are at the very bottom, and those things despised and trampled upon and dumped at the bottom of the world's ladder are the top rungs of God's ladder.

The things God's followers pursue are all the things that the world deems unimportant. So we are living right-side up in an upside-down world.

People around you don't understand. While you are pursuing faith and meekness, forgiveness and love and humility, they feel that you are going down the ladder into the mire of failure and worthlessness. You are not in the struggle; you are not in the rat race. You are swimming upstream, against the stream of the world.

When you get a glimpse of the purpose of God for your life, your whole perspective changes. Your whole value system changes. Your whole reward system changes. What's important is turned upside down. That is what Jesus does when He comes into your life. He enters your life and turns it upside down. But, really, what He's doing is turning it right-side up. It just looks like it's upside down to everyone else.

People look at you, puzzled, and say, "What do you mean, you don't do that anymore? What do you mean you are trusting God? What do you mean you are going to pray about it? What's that kind of stuff?" Our whole perspective changes when we get a glimpse of the purpose of God.

Romans 8:28 says, "We know that all things work together for good to those who love God." All things work. That means the good things and the bad things; not one thing in particular.

We Must Live Purposely, in God's Purpose

We must live purposefully. We can't live by accident. We can't live from situation to situation, from circumstance to circumstance. We live with a deliberate purpose in mind. We have a course.

Paul said, "I have finished my course." He was on course; from the time he met Christ, his course began.

All things work together for good. But not just for any good. Scripture says they work together for the good of those that are the called *according to his purpose* (Rom. 8:28).

So, then, it must be imperative and extremely important that we find out what that purpose is, what the purpose of God is for our lives.

Second Timothy 1:9 (NKJV) says this: "[He] has saved us and called us with a holy calling, not according to our works, but according to his own purpose and grace, which was given to us in Christ Jesus." He called us, not according to our own works but according to His own purpose.

God measures our life in terms of purpose. Not in terms of time. Ecclesiastes 3:1 says, "To everything there is a season, and a time for every purpose under heaven."

God will always give and make time for our purpose to be accomplished.

Don't say that you are too old. Don't say that you have waited too long. God will make time for you to fulfill your purpose because God does not measure your life in terms of how old you are; He measures your life in terms of your purpose. Moses was eighty years old before God began to use him.

Everything in life has a purpose. And so, God, who is the master designer, had a purpose when He created you. He didn't just put you here for nothing. He made you the way you were, designed you, put you in the family you're in, allowed you to experience all that you experience—with a purpose in mind.

How could God just keep on making people and not give each one a purpose? The sun has a purpose. The stars have a purpose. The birds have a purpose. Trees have a purpose. Everything has this magnificent design to it that God created. So how could His crowning creation (Psalm 8) not have purpose?

All things begin and end with a purpose. So, fulfilling your purpose must become the primary goal in your life. Because in fulfilling the purpose that God created you for brings glory to God.

Don't Abuse Your Purpose

When you don't know your purpose, you are spinning your wheels. Time is being wasted in your life because you are fluttering all over, but you are not fulfilling your purpose.

And when you do not fulfill your purpose, abuse occurs.

The word *abuse* comes from two words: "abnormal use." When you don't know what the purpose of a thing is, abuse is inevitable.

For instance, when my kids were young, I came in their bedroom and they were turning flips on the bed. *Boing, boing, boing!* And I said, "Listen, that's not the purpose of the bed. The purpose of the bed is for sleeping." But they were getting good use out of the bed; it was working pretty good! But that is not what it was made for.

There are a lot of things we don't use purposefully. Someone said that the Hope Diamond was a doorstop for many years before someone noticed it was a diamond and realized how valuable it was. When we do not understand the purpose of a thing, we will abuse it.

I read a story of two men who had a hedge between their houses, and they were too cheap to buy a hedge trimmer. So they would get on each side of the hedge and hold up their lawnmowers to try to cut it. One of the men cut his finger off and sued the lawnmower company. Well, that was not the intended purpose for the lawnmower. The lawnmower was created to cut lawns.

We must understand that when we do not use our lives as intended, abuse becomes inevitable. If you do not know the proper use of drugs—and, of course, God created all of the herbs that we make drugs from—you will have drug abuse.

Now, I would not go see my dentist if she didn't have some drugs in her cabinet. I don't care how much faith you have—I don't care how much you love God, or how much you are fasting and praying—you are not going to drill my teeth for cavities without giving me a shot of Novocain.

I love the Lord; I'm a man of faith; I trust God. But I want Novocain when I go to the dentist. There is nothing wrong with using drugs as God created and purposed them to be used. But when you use them for the wrong purpose, that's abuse.

When you don't know the purpose of your wife or the purpose of your husband, you have spousal abuse. When you don't know why God gave you children and you don't understand the purpose of your children and your purpose in their lives, you have child abuse. They are not being used for the purpose for which they were designed or created.

Many of us wasted a lot of years in abuse. I was a drug abuser. I abused my life for all those years in wrongdoing and the criminal activities that I was involved in, in the early years of my life. I didn't know what my life was for. I didn't have a clue.

It's so important that we find purpose. Because everything that God does begins and ends with a purpose. Purpose reveals to us the reasons behind life's experiences. Life's demands. It gives us vision for the future. We are given significance because we are here for a purpose. We are valuable. We were designed. God wants to use us.

Ask Your Maker

If you want to know the purpose of a product, you go to the manufacturer, right? If I want to know what's wrong with my smartphone, I look at the manual. I can't use the one for my previous phone because it has different features and buttons. I have to get the instructions for this phone.

We go to the source to begin to discover our purpose. To the one who put us together, so that we can understand and discover our purpose. That discovery process begins and ends with our relationship with Jesus Christ. Through the Word and prayer, we understand our purpose.

The Bible says in Proverbs 20:18, "Every purpose is established by counsel." Whom do we consult with in discovering our purpose? Well, first and foremost, we consult with God. We ask, "God, why did you make me? What is my purpose? Reveal to me your will, Lord."

We can't always run to the Bible, though. You can run to the Bible to understand some things, but you can't run to the Bible to find out whether you should marry Tim or Jerry. You can't run to the Bible and say, "Should I take that job over at Hewlett-Packard and leave my job at IBM?" You can't run to your Bible and ask, "Should I get the Toyota or should I go with the Nissan?" You can't run to the Bible and ask, "What church should I attend?"

Now, we can surely get counsel and understanding from the Bible, but we also have to learn how to hear the voice of God. How do you determine the will of God? How do you know the will of God?

How to Determine the Will of God

First, you ask God outright. Just ask Him outright through prayer: "Lord, what is your will for my life?" Just like that.

Second, you search the Scriptures. You pore over the Scriptures; you may not get a specific "Tim" or "Jerry," but you will get an idea of the mind of God concerning your situation. You can find counsel and guidelines and parameters for God's will in your life, and in certain instances you can get specifics right from the Word of God.

So you seek God in prayer. You search the Scriptures.

Third, you seek out wise counsel. You go to those in the body of Christ where you are in fellowship, and you ask, "Can you help me to determine the will of God? Do you have any counsel for me? You have observed my life. Here's my situation—can you give me wise counsel on this?"

You can get other counsel, too, from your parents or from a friend or a prayer partner. Seek out wise counselors. Elders in the church, people in your life who are significant and who are role models.

Fourth, you consider the circumstances. Let's say you wake up one morning and say, "I think I'll go buy a brand-new Rolls Royce."

Well, you had better consider your circumstances. Do you have the money to buy a Rolls Royce?

You say, "God called me to the ministry. I'm going to quit my job and just go full-time into the ministry." Oh, and you have a couple of kids to feed, a house note, a husband or wife to consult with. You have to consider the circumstances.

Circumstances do not make our decision for us. But we must consider the circumstances. God often helps to guide us in that manner. "I have responsibilities. I must do this. I can't just leave and go to India tomorrow."

The fifth step requires you come to a conclusion. This step in determining the will of God is the hardest. After you have prayed, searched the Scriptures, sought out wise counsel, and considered the circumstances, you now must come to a conclusion. You have weighed all these things, and you are saying to God, "Father, to the best of my ability in understanding your will in this circumstance, this is what I believe that you want me to do," and then you do it.

See, if we do not take that final step—that leap of faith—then we are always teetering, and we never move forward. We learn and grow and mature through trial and error.

You'll Still Make Mistakes

You are still going to make some mistakes. And you are going to keep learning from the mistakes you make. Even if you read the Bible every day and fast three times a month and pray incessantly, you are going to make some mistakes.

And that's why you take your ministry seriously, but you don't take yourself too seriously. If you do, you won't last long. I guarantee it.

You'd better learn to laugh at yourself. Ask any preacher. Sometimes I get up, think that since I've studied all week I have the mind of God, then I get ready to preach, and nothing comes together. I'm thinking, "I'll be glad when this service is over so I can go home and get out of here."

Then there are other times when I haven't prepared. I've been so busy that I just flew in and I'm tired. God gave me a verse when I woke up and I had a thought on it, and that's all. Yet, when I get to the pulpit, the words flow and everyone is blessed by the talk. God just wants me to know that it has nothing to do with me.

I remember telling the Lord a couple of years ago, "God, I'm not doing anything right, and the church is still growing and you're blessing. Oh, you know what? It's your grace! It has to be your grace because I haven't done anything right."

You'll make some mistakes, but you must come to some conclusion and say, "God, to the best of my ability to understand, this is what I believe you want me to do."

I guarantee you, God will honor it even if you do the wrong thing. Because He will say, "He made his choice based on this," and He will somehow bring you to the place where He desires you to be.

Every purpose is established by counsel. But we're going to make mistakes in the spirit.

The Bible tells us in Revelation 1 how the apostle John "was in the spirit on the Lord's Day." He says, "I heard a voice behind me saying 'I am the Alpha and Omega, the beginning and the end.'"

So, here John's in the spirit, right? Further on, in chapter 4 it says, "And I heard the voice of a trumpet calling unto me and it said, 'come up hither,' and immediately, I was in the spirit. . . . And I was caught up and I saw a throne," and he starts penning what he sees.

At one point he's so blown away by what he sees, he bows down to worship an angel. Mistake!

The angel says, "No, don't worship me. I am your fellow servant. Worship Jesus."

John makes a mistake. He's in the heavenly realm, and he makes a mistake.

So, here on earth, we're going to make some mistakes. But we learn from them. And God will teach us—probably more from our mistakes than from our successes.

To know our purpose, we must determine the will of God and do it. And every purpose is established by counsel. First you counsel with God. Then you talk to the teachers that you've had in ministry in your church who have observed you and worked with you. You talk to your parents, if they are believers. Or to your pastor.

And then you move forward, in faith, in purpose.

Chapter 7: God Bestows Gifts

God has given us gifts—talents and skills. Gifts are given by the spirit of God. Talents are given by God at birth. Some people are born with a talent to sing, to pick up a pencil and draw, to play music. They are birthed with talent.

Skills are learned. They take commitment and hard work. You might be born with a gift to play the piano, and someone else might have to take lessons and work hard to learn to play the piano. You both can play the piano. In either case, God wants us to fulfill our purpose by using our gifts, talents, and skills.

There are different types of gifts God bestows on people. The first are office gifts, which are listed in Ephesians chapter 4. "But to each one of us grace was given according to the measure of Christ's gift. . . . And He Himself gave to some to be apostles, some prophets, some evangelists, and some pastors and teachers" (verses 7 and 11, NKJV). These are what we commonly known as the office gifts.

They are sometimes referred to as the fivefold ministry. Look at your hand. The thumb speaks of the apostle; he touches all the other ministries—gives direction, covering oversight for them all.

The first finger speaks of the prophet. He's always pointing out, pointing things right, things wrong.

Your middle finger speaks of the evangelist. It's the longest finger on your hand. The evangelist goes out; he reaches out the furthest; he travels.

Your ring finger on your hand speaks of the pastor.

This finger and the vein in this finger are tied directly to your heart. It's the weakest finger on your hand, and it's the finger you put your ring on. In comparison, the pastor is married to the church.

And the littlest finger speaks of the teacher. Notice when your ear itches, this is the one that gets furthest into the ear. The teacher gets to your ear and builds structure inside. This is an easy way to remember the fivefold ministry.

God Bestows Spiritual Gifts

A second group of gifts is found in 1 Corinthians 12:4–11. In this passage, we find our spiritual gifts, or the gifts of the spirit. "There are diversities of gifts, but the same spirit. There are differences of ministries, but the same Lord."

In other words, there are different gifts, but it's the same spirit. There are differences in the way they are administrated.

Though some may have the same gift, it does not come across the same way. There are different ways that the word of knowledge or word of wisdom comes across. But it's the same God who works all in all. "But the manifestation of the spirit is given to each one, to profit all." Gifts are never for our own use.

> For to one is given word of wisdom through the spirit; to another, word of knowledge to the same spirit; to another, faith by the same spirit; to another, gifts of healings by the same spirit; to another, the working of miracles; to another, prophecy; to another, discerning of spirits; to another, different kinds of tongues or diverse tongues, and to another interpretation of tongues. But one and the same spirit works all of these, distributing to each one individually as he wills.

Revelation Gifts

The gifts of the spirit are often divided into three categories. First are the "revelation" gifts. Gifts that reveal wisdom or knowledge or insights. The word of wisdom generally speaks of the future, of instruction regarding something that you should do. It is not the entire wisdom of God; it is a portion of the wisdom of God that is given.

God knows everything, and when we receive a word of knowledge, we receive a portion of the knowledge of God. It generally deals with what has happened in the past or what is going on in the present.

Then we have the gift of discerning spirits. That is the ability to discern what spirit is in operation. There are three spirits that are generally in operation—a satanic spirit, a divine spirit—the Holy Spirit—or the human spirit.

Know that sometimes people are just speaking out of their heart. It doesn't have anything to do with God—they are just emotionally moved. You understand that is the human spirit. But sometimes the Enemy is on the move. Oftentimes someone will see clearly what spirit is in operation. This is the gift of discerning spirits.

Now, don't think you have to have this gift to have discernment. All believers get discernment when they are born again, and you should hone and develop and mature your discernment so that you can know what is true and not true. You should have discernment working in your life.

Power Gifts

In addition to these kinds of "revelation" gifts, there are the "power" gifts. These are gifts that do something. The gift of faith, which is generally passive, believes God. It doesn't necessarily do anything.

The working of miracles is an active gift. You are involved: stretch forth your rod.

Then there are the gifts of healings. Those provide healing for the physical, healing for the emotional, and healing for spiritual hurts as well. We've seen the gifts of healings in operation. Some people are more successful in one area of healing than others.

In the old days, Oral Roberts would lay hands on everyone, and God would heal. Kathryn Kuhlman would come out with all these beautiful gowns on, and through a word of knowledge, gifts of healings were operating. She would say, "In the balcony, there, I see the Holy Spirit healing. Right here, I see the Holy Spirit healing."

She never worked up a sweat; Oral Roberts would be soaking wet. It doesn't make one better than the other; it just means God uses different people in different ways.

Jesus often used a combination of gifts at one time. At the tomb of Lazarus, He had to have faith to call Lazarus's name. He had to perform a miracle for Lazarus to get up. And when Lazarus got up, he had to be healed so he wouldn't die again.

And so there are many gifts, oftentimes, that are working in conjunction with one another. Those are power gifts. Gifts that do something.

Vocal Gifts and Motivational Gifts

Then there are three vocal gifts: gifts that say something. Prophecy, which gives direction and instruction and can speak to the future. And diverse kinds of tongues and interpretation of those tongues. Those are the gifts that were birthed on the day of Pentecost, and they are the introduction to New Testament life. On the day of Pentecost, they all spoke in the spirit of God, and they were gathered together.

Then there are the seven motivational gifts. The list is found in Romans 12, beginning with verse 6. It says:

Having, then, gifts differing according to the grace which is given us, let us use them. If prophecy, let us prophesy in the proportion to our faith. Or ministry, let us use it for ministry. He who teaches, in teaching. He who exhorts, in exhortation. He who gives, with liberality. He who leads, with diligence. He who shows mercy, with cheerfulness. (NKJV)

These are called the motivational gifts because they are what turn us on. They are what motivate us. They get us excited and going. There are those who are motivated by teaching. And there are those who are motivated by giving. Those who are motivated by mercy.

It's important that you discover what your motivational gift is and what gifts are active in your life. I used to think, "Well, gee, my motivational gift is teaching." But the more I looked and the more God began to deal with me, the more I realized my motivational gift is exhortation. I just prefer exhorting people. Teaching is one of the minor gifts that I have, but I love exhortation. I love encouraging people. That's what energizes me. Making the Word of God practical.

And so you find out what your motivational gift is. And then other gifts are listed in 1 Corinthians 12:28 that involve helping others and administrating or leading.

The Bible refers to the gift of celibacy. Wow. Every single has the gift of celibacy until they get married. But then there are those who never get married and are perfectly fulfilled in their lives. Paul, we are told, had the gift of celibacy. He says, "I wish that all of you were as I am." And most of us say, "No, we don't." Paul says, in essence, "It's good for a man not to touch a woman. But, you know, if you can't help yourself, then get married" (1 Cor. 7:6–7).

There's a gift of hospitality. People who love to bring people in and to work behind the scenes and take care of them. Martha, Jesus's friend, had that gift (Luke 10).

Some even have the gift of martyrdom. That's a gift you use one time.

Some have the gift of missionary service and are led to live in a foreign country. They go abroad and unpack their bags, living in a land with different food, different water, different culture, different everything. They are not blown away by it; they do not lose their focus. They know why they are there: to present the gospel of Jesus Christ.

Not everyone can go to the mission field and stay. Not everyone is gifted to make that transition.

Billy Graham's wife was born and raised in China. Her parents were missionaries. She was educated in China. I had a friend who took his wife and two children and moved to South Africa with Overseas Crusades, to live and work there. I have a friend that we support in Nairobi. He graduated from University of Chicago. His wife is from Chicago. But they live in Kenya with their two children. They speak Swahili fluently, and they are just marvelous there. Another missionary, who our church supports, is Ruth Applewhite, and she is a very good friend of mine. I do not know a more powerful woman, yet she is very quiet. She has worked in Haiti ever since I became a Christian, more than three decades that she has been there. And God uses her. I had strep throat when visiting her, and I had to preach that morning, and she just came in and prayed quietly, "Lord, just touch . . ." I was healed instantly. Just like that. What a powerful woman. When she prays, you almost quake, but she doesn't make any noise. A lot of people don't know her. And that's the gift of the missionary.

And then there is the gift of voluntary poverty. You might laugh, but it's a gifting to move into the inner city, to move into a place that is devastatingly poor, and live among the poor instead of across town. Instead of coming to minister every morning and then, when you get through, going to your nice warm home with a full refrigerator.

Those with that kind of gift are there in the midst of the suffering and are part of the community. They aren't aiming for worldly fame, money, or fortune, and they feel fulfilled and effective in their calling.

1 Corinthians 13 tells us if we don't have love, we have nothing. But there are those who give all their goods away. I know some right here in San Jose, California, who were owners of companies and managers and in high positions, and they gave that all up to go work for Cityteam or some other street ministry, and they are much more fulfilled now in their lives.

Chapter 8: Seven Pillars of Wisdom

Divine purpose and design are to operate in every area of your life—not just at home. They flow into your marriage, the way you raise your kids, and the way you get along with people. Real wisdom causes our lives to line up with the purpose of God for us. We line up with the purpose of God in every area of our life.

Proverbs 9:1 says, "Wisdom has built her house, and she has hewn out her seven pillars." Wisdom's house is built on seven pillars. And real wisdom involves living according to God's purpose for your life. That is probably the best definition of wisdom. Why would I try to be someone else and struggle all my life? Why don't I find the purpose of God, line up everything in my life with it, and live according to God's purpose? If I do that, I will be fulfilled, and God will be glorified.

Wisdom's seven pillars are the seven areas of our life that we need to align with God's Word in terms of our purpose. Let's take a look at each one of them.

First and foremost is our spiritual pillar. We line our life up spiritually, and understand our purpose spiritually, and live according to that purpose.

The second pillar is our mental capacity. We need to *understand* the purpose of God. We need to educate ourselves. We need to get our minds on the things above. Christianity is more than just emotion; it's cerebral. God wants people who think. Who are healthy mentally.

The third pillar concerns our physical body. When we are tired physically, we don't do much praying. We don't do much serving. We don't do much thinking. We don't do much reading. We don't do much of anything when we are tired. We just go to sleep. If we're out of shape, we put out minimal effort and then get tired. How can God use us?

Therefore, we need to align our life physically with God. That doesn't mean you have to look like a model on the cover of a sports magazine. But you should have a healthy diet; you should exercise; you should do what's needed so that you can live a long life and be healthy. Then, when God puts His hand on you, you can be used by God.

The fourth pillar involves our social life. In terms of both the world and the church, we need to be aware socially of what is going on in our community and what needs there are. What good is it to come to church and pray and not recognize that there are drugs in our community, that homes are falling apart in our community? We need to pay attention to the relationships we make in our church, the friendships we develop, and the needs that require attention in the body of Christ. We need to line up our lives socially with the purposes of God.

The fifth pillar involves our vocation. What are you going to do for the rest of your life? It's important that we understand that so we don't end up working a job that we hate. If that's your situation now, don't let it stay that way. Talk with a counselor; talk with someone at church. Find out what you are gifted at. Go back to school if you have to; go at night if you need to keep your day job.

When I went back to school for my AA, I was in my thirties and had four children. I had to go to school at night and on weekends. I was determined to get my AA. When I committed to getting my bachelor of theology degree, I had to take classes on Mondays, all day, and some weekends and evenings.

When I worked on my master's, I was pastoring a church. Had the same four kids, but they were older. I love learning, and I want to be able to stretch what I can do.

Find vocationally what you love to do. If you have to go back to school, do it, so that you can do the will of God and be fulfilled in your work.

The sixth pillar concerns our finances. We need to find the purpose of God for our finances. God doesn't want us to stress, worry about paying our rent each month or our bills, unable to sleep, gripped by fear and trepidation concerning our finances.

You want to know the key to wealth? Save more than you spend. It's that simple, but there is a process for doing that. Get someone to help you budget and understand your finances and how to manage your spending. If you have a bit of savings, learn what investments you could make.

The seventh pillar of wisdom is all about relationship. That has to do with our family. Our parents, and our relationship with them. Our relationship with our spouses. Our relationship with our children. And if you are single, how you carry yourself in your singleness in terms of the relationships that you have.

Our lives, in these seven areas, should be aligned with the purpose of God. Philippians 2:12–13 says, "Work out your own salvation with fear and trembling." Work out the purposes of God, your own salvation, with fear and trembling, "for it is God that works in you, both to will and to do his good pleasure."

We must work it out. I don't know how you are going to work out your finances. I don't know how you are going to work out your marriage. I don't know how you will work out, but you, with the help of the spirit of God, will be living in wisdom because you will be aligning every area of your life according to the purposes of God.

Psalm 119:164 says, "Seven times a day, I praise you because of your righteous judgements." There are seven areas of my life in which I can give God glory for every day, because they are all submitted to Him and they are all moving according to the purpose of God. We shouldn't have a hard time finding something to give God praise and honor and glory for.

Discover the purpose of God in your life. Ask God outright. Search the Scriptures. Understand the gifts that God gives. Understand the gifts that you have been a recipient of. Understand the talents that God has placed in your life. Understand what motivates you. What gets you going?

I love, and have for decades, to go visit the prison. I love it. I love to preach at San Quentin more than I love to preach at my church. We have a great time out there. There are other people who, when I say, "Come on, let's go to the jail," they say, "Oh, no, I don't want to go inside the jail. I don't like to hear those doors slam." I can't get mad at them and say, "You guys are not really Christians."

In my case, I have the most difficult time going to the hospital, to the rest homes, to visit older people. I don't do very well. I do it; it's part of my ministry, but it's not my favorite thing to do. But I have a deacon who loves to go. He loves walking around the convalescent home, bringing cheer. What a wonderful ministry! He understands his gifting and his purpose.

Some people are gifted to work with couples; some people are not. My wife, when we started the church, went in with the children on Friday night, and that night, she said, "That is not my ministry." At the time she had our four kids at home, and maybe that was enough. But some are gifted to work with children. And so we accept each other as we are.

God sets us in the church as He wills. He gives gifts according to his will. Discover your gift and your purpose from God.

Everything you do, you do by faith. "The just shall live by faith" (Hab. 2:4). There's nothing written that is going to tell you how to live next year. If someone had told me what was going to happen when I started pastoring, I would have turned the job down and said, "No way." But now, looking back, I see no other way that God could have taught me and brought me. I'm so glad that He did that.

Seek God out and determine that purpose. It is part of your design and your makeup. Find out what you like to do. Take every area of your life and determine God's purpose. And by faith you will continue to move forward, and God will use you greatly. You can count on it.

The Fourth "P" – Performance

It's one thing to know that God has called you to do something with your life, but it's a whole other thing to perform that purpose—that's where the rubber meets the road.

Chapter 9: God's Purpose Leads to Performance

We first must understand who we are. We must understand our position and our place in Christ, and where we are in our own hearts. We must discover and find our purpose, and then we must, after finding our purpose, begin to carry it out through to completion. In other words: finish the course. What good does it do to ask God to show you His purpose for your life and then you don't do anything? Your performance is your response to God's purpose for your life.

In Luke 1:45 (KJV), it says, concerning Mary, the mother of Jesus, "Blessed is she who believed, for there will be a performance of those things which were told her from the Lord." Some translations say "a fulfillment" instead of a performance. When we believe God, there will be a performance of what God said.

Gabriel came with an impossible message to Mary, an impossible circumstance and situation for her. And not only impossible but potentially embarrassing. "You are going to become pregnant, and you're not even going to know a man." Right. Okay. She could have run from it; she could have shrunk from it. But she said, "Lord, let it be to me even as you have said." The angel tells her, in essence, "You are going to bear the Messiah. The Son of God is going to be birthed from your womb. The Ancient of Days is going to become a baby, and you are going to care for Him and raise Him. The Holy Spirit will overshadow you, and the thing that will be conceived in you shall be holy, even God." She believed God's purpose for her life. And the Scripture says she was blessed, "because there shall be a performance of those things that were told her of the Lord."

Let me give you an equation: what you believe plus what you value equals what you do. The key is that your values are stronger than your beliefs. Your values are more powerful than what you believe. That's why we can look at a person who really loves the Lord, who believes the Scriptures, who does not doubt God, but not see anything produced in their life. We see believers who value the wrong things, and their values override what they believe.

Take David, for instance. He never stopped believing God. He knew that God was the King of Israel. He knew that God's word was true. Just check out the psalms. Just check out David's life. There is never a time when he doubted God was sovereign. But one afternoon, he valued a little time with Bathsheba more than his belief in God's sovereignty. David knew it was wrong. He had penned:

> If I go up to heaven, you are there; if I go down to the grave, you are there. If I ride the wings of the morning, if I dwell by the farthest oceans, even there your hand will guide me, and your strength will support me. I could ask the darkness to hide me and the light around me to become night—but even in darkness I cannot hide from you. To you the night shines as bright as day. Darkness and light are the same to you. (Psalm 139:8–12 NLT)

You can turn out the lights, and God can still see what you are doing. David valued something more than what he believed. And so he sinned with Bathsheba.

There are struggling addicts who really love the Lord, but they keep falling. I don't doubt that they love the Lord and believe the Bible, and believe that Jesus Christ died for their sins.

But they value something more than what they believe. Jesus put it like this: "For where your treasure is, there your heart will be also" (Matt. 6:21 NKJV).

There is an awful lot of talking and little doing. God complained that His people served Him with their lips, but their heart was far removed from Him (Isa. 29:13). When you start valuing something over God, it will swing you away from what you believe, and that is why you must value, above everything, your relationship with Christ.

What you value will dictate what you do. When you value what you believe, you will perform the will of God. You must value your relationship with Jesus Christ, and you must value the purpose of God in your life above everything else. And then you will see, by your behavior, the will of God being performed in your life, because you are going to do it.

Psalm 61:8 says, "That I might daily perform my vows." That means every day we value the will of God. If we value prayer, what are we going to do? We are going to pray. If we value the Word of God, what are we going to do? We are going to hide it in our hearts.

It doesn't take much to look at where you spend most of your energy. Churches are filled with believers, but one poll I read says about 10 percent of parishioners do 100 percent of the work. People flood in on Sunday; they hear the message; they get in their cars, and they are gone. There is a core group that continues to minister. Jesus understood this. He said, "The harvest truly is plentiful, but the laborers are few" (Matt. 9:37 NKJV). We have plenty of Pharisees and Sadducees; we have plenty of lawyers and scribes; we have plenty of reverends and deacons. The harvest is plentiful, but the laborers, the ones who will roll their sleeves up and perform the will of God under the strength and power of the Holy Spirit, are few. Jesus urged: "Pray to the Lord of the harvest to send out laborers into His harvest" (verse 38).

Psalm 119:112 (NKJV) says, "I have inclined my heart to perform Your statutes, forever to the very end." We need to tell God, "I'm going to perform your statutes to the very end. I have inclined my heart. I have set my heart to perform what your Word has laid out for me to the very end."

I love Jesus's statement in John 4:34. He says, "My food is to do the will of Him that sent me" (NKJV). What sustains me, what feeds me, what gives me strength and energy, what refreshes me and establishes me and nurtures my heart and my soul and my spirit—that fulfills me. To perform the purpose of God in my life—that is what satisfies me.

Jesus's disciples come back from buying bread after Jesus won the heart of the woman at the Samaritan well, having talked to her. One woman. And eventually she tells the whole city. The disciples urge Him to eat, and He says, in essence, "I am already full. I have food you know not of. There's something else that satisfies me. There is something else that fulfills my hunger pains. And that's to do the will of Him that sent me. To perform the purpose that Father sent me to perform." In John 8:29 (KJV), He says, "I always do those things that please him." He says "I always do." Not always think about. Not always hope for. But "I always do the things that please him."

We go to God and say, "I need an adjustment because my behavior does not line up with what I realize is your purpose for me." I don't want to be a misbehaving believer. I don't want to miss what God wants me to do.

I know that God loves me in spite of my misbehavior. I love the old nursery song that says, "Jesus loves me, this I know, for the Bible tells me so." The second stanza says, "Jesus loves me when I'm good, and I do the things I should. And He loves me when I'm bad, but it makes Him very sad. Yes, Jesus loves me." Yes, He loves us when we are misbehaving. Yes, He loves us when we are not fulfilling the purposes of God, and that's great. We thank God for the wonderful grace, but I want to do the will of God. Not so that He will love me; He loves me already. I want to do it so He will be glorified in my life, and so that I will be fulfilled.

I am not driven by rules and regulations; because I know Him, because He has given me purpose, I want to fulfill the purpose of God so that He can be glorified.

And so my motivation is faith that works through love. Because I love Him, I am going to do the will of God. Because I love Him, I trust Him with my life. I know He will not let me down, so I will step out of the boat onto the water. I will do the will of God. I will perform the purpose of God. There will be the performance of God's purpose in my life.

Not only must we know what to do, we must do it. Do it. Perform the purpose of God.

The Fifth "P" – Product

When we've positioned ourselves so that God can use us, our lives should then be productive. Something should come forth that will bring God praise.

Chapter 10: Produce Much Fruit

To produce means to bring forth. It is your result of doing the will of God. What are the results when you do the will of God? What results when you have obeyed God, when you have found your purpose, and you have performed your purpose? We are always being put together; we are always getting a little more understanding; we are always praying more; we are always being helped and encouraged more; we are always being trained and taught more, and we are always serving God. What is the result of the assembly line of our lives?

That which we produce, the Scriptures speak of as "fruit." The fruit that I produce is the result of my life. Let's take a look at chapter 15 of the gospel of John. In verse 8 (ESV), Jesus says, "By this my Father is glorified: that you bear much fruit and so prove to be my disciples."

If you really want to know how to glorify God in your life, in your ministries, in the things you do and say, in your relationships, Jesus essentially says, "Let me pull it all together for you. This is how my Father is glorified: bear much fruit."

In Genesis 1:28, we read how God created man in his image. Note how the first words He utters to Adam are "Be fruitful and multiply." Be productive.

In Genesis chapter 9, after God destroys the world with water and preserves Noah and his wife and children, the ark lands on Mt. Ararat, and in verse 1 God blesses Noah and his sons and says this to him: "Be fruitful and multiply and fill the earth."

God gets glory out of our lives when we are productive. God does not get glory out of anything that just sits dormant, that does not grow or produce anything, does not have anything to show for an encounter with Him.

God is after a people that will be productive. When we were created, part of His purpose for us is that we would be productive. Ephesians 2:10 (NIV) says: "For we are God's handiwork, created in Christ Jesus to do good works, which God prepared in advance for us to do."

To be fruitful means to grow. It means to increase, be productive. Jesus is saying, "My Father is glorified when you are growing, when there is increase, when you are bringing forth, when your life is productive." To glorify God means giving Him the full honor that belongs to Him.

Now what do we mean when we say "be productive"? Fruit is the visible expression of the power of God working inwardly and invisibly in our lives. It is the manifestation, the expression, that God is alive, that He is at work in my life, the Spirit of God abides in me.

In John 15:7 (NKJV), Jesus says "If you abide in Me and My words abide in you, you will ask what you desire, and it shall be done for you." There is an abiding that takes place, and if God is abiding in our lives, if He is at work in our lives, if He is who He said He is, if He is doing what He promised He would do, if He is to us what He has promised He would be, and if we are to Him what He created us to be, then we are going to be fruitful.

And there is going to be a visible expression in your life that God is at work in you, even though you cannot see it visibly. He is at work inside, causing us to will and to act (Phil. 2:13). To be fruitful.

Look at John 15:16. Jesus says to his disciples, "You didn't choose me, but I chose you and appointed you" (NIV). Some translations say, "I ordained you."

"Why did you ordain me, God?"

"That you should go forth and bear fruit."

Has God changed anything here? From Genesis to the New Testament, written thousands of years later, He speaks the same words: "I chose you. I ordained you and I appointed you, that you should go and bear fruit, and that your fruit should remain. And whatever you ask the Father in my name, He may give it to you." Prayer is linked to our productiveness. Jesus says, "Bear fruit as you go; bear fruit and you will ask the Father and he will give it to you."

Jesus says, "If you ask anything in my name, I will do it." Well, suppose I hired you and told you, "Listen, I want you to go to my house and live there. I've got weeds in the backyard, so I'm hiring you to knock down all those weeds. Weed whacker's in the backyard. Just go take care of that—I appreciate it. And if you need anything, you can reach me at the office. If you need anything, anything at all, just call me. And I'll see that you get it."

So you go over to my house, and you're whacking down the weeds, and you get to thinking, "Wow. Anything? If I need anything . . ." *Ring, ring.* "Hello, Tony?"

"Yes. How's it going over at the house?"

"Oh, fine. I'm about halfway done. But you said if I needed anything to call you."

"Of course. What do you need?"

"Um, I need a new house, and I need a new car. And, you know, I could use a new wardrobe. And I really need a vacation; I really need to go to Hawaii for a couple of weeks."

"What are you talking about?"

"Well, you said, if I need anything, just call you."

And I say, "No, you don't understand. If you needed anything *to get the job done* that I sent you to do, then call."

We cannot take God's words out of context. Sometimes we ask for something, and we figure if it comes, fine; if it doesn't, that will be okay. We'll live without it.

That's no way to have a relationship. If you need a Cadillac to get the job done that God sent you to do, then He will give you one. You need a house way up on a hill and beautiful furniture to accomplish what God has asked you to do, no problem.

But you can't just tell God, "Oh, I want you to do this, and I want you to do that and get that for me."

He is not a spiritual butler; He is not a kind of Holy Ghost Santa Claus or a divine vending machine. Prayer is tied to our fulfilling our appointment and our ordination. "I have chosen you for myself, and I have ordained you and appointed you that you would go forth and bear fruit."

Prayer is tied to our being productive. If your young son says, "I want to play the guitar, Dad," and you buy him a little toy guitar that's inexpensive, and he starts strumming it, but then you see the thing stuffed under his bed, or he's batting tennis balls with it in the backyard, and he hasn't played it in six weeks. And then he comes to you and says, "Hey, you know what? I really want one of those Fender guitars. You know—the ones that cost thousands of dollars with a great big amp?"

Well, you're not going to be motivated to buy that expensive guitar for him because he hasn't been productive with what you already gave him.

Why would God give us all we request if we are not productive? If we are faithful in a little, He will reward us with much (Luke 16:10).

What do we mean by "faithful"? We want to be productive with what we have. God is not asking you to bear any more fruit than what He has planted in your life.

God knows the seed that was planted; He knows the gifts and talents He has planted in you. He asks you to be fruitful with what He has given you.

He has chosen you and ordained you, that you go forth and bring forth fruit.

We All Must Be Pruned

Fruitfulness is a process. Let's go back to John 15, beginning with verse 1 (NKJV). "I am the true vine; and My Father is the vinedresser. Every branch in Me that does not bear fruit He takes away." Wow. He's pretty serious about you bearing some fruit, isn't He? "And every branch that bears fruit He prunes."

As we become productive, there are some things that need to be cut off so that we can become more productive. Anyone who has grown fruit trees or rosebushes knows that you prune them. If you have a fruit tree with too many limbs, you get tiny fruit because they are all competing for water and nourishment. So you cut a few limbs, and the result is larger, more voluptuous, and better fruit—and a better-producing tree.

If we overcommit, spread ourselves too thin, run around everywhere, without focus to our lives, not knowing what our purpose is or what God called us to do, what we produce is going to be anemic and lacking, and God is not going to get much glory out of our lives.

So, the first thing Jesus says is that every branch must bear fruit. But He is going to prune it, because He wants to take you to the next level, which will generate more fruit. First you bear fruit, then God will hone you, your gifts and talents.

When you first find your gift and your purpose, you use it clumsily. You do the best you can, but the more you do it, the more you hone your purpose. You get better and better at being who God created you to be, better at your purpose as you understand and perform your purpose. Now you're not just bearing fruit, you are bearing *more* fruit.

Jesus says in verse 4, "Abide in Me and I in you, as the branch cannot bear fruit of itself." Listen, you cannot do anything on your own. If you are going to be productive, it is going to take that relationship with the Lord. "As the branch cannot bear fruit of itself, unless it abides in the vine, neither can you unless you abide in Me." That word *abide* means "to stay."

Jesus says that when we abide in Him, we produce much fruit." But apart from Him, we can produce nothing (verse 5). Do nothing. Accomplish nothing. To have a product that pleases God, that lies within His will, we have to abide.

What if we really lived our lives based on what Jesus said right here? If we lived by the truth that "apart from Him, you can do nothing." We were not made to accomplish anything apart from Him. Not anything that is of any real benefit or lasting meaning to the kingdom of God.

In Matthew 7:16, Jesus makes an interesting statement: "You shall know them by their fruit." While we don't go around judging people, by the fruit produced, we can identify people in relationship with God who know their purpose, who understand their calling, who are performing the purpose of God, and, as a result of that wonderful relationship with God, are bearing fruit.

And it's not all about ministry. Are you fruitful and productive in your family? Is your marriage fruitful and productive? Is your relationship with your kids productive? Is your relationship with your friends productive? Are the things you do on your job, when you are working and interacting with your coworkers, productive?

We need to ask: Is God glorified at every level of my life? Am I productive in every level of my life? "Product" is not always something tangible—something you can hold in your hands. Galatians 6:7 says, "Do not be deceived; God is not mocked; for whatever a man sows, that he will also reap" (NKJV). If you sow to the flesh, you are going to reap corruption. If you sow to the spirit, you will reap life everlasting. Fullness.

In order to bear fruit, you must finish what God has given you to do. You must perform your purpose continually. Run the race to the finish line (1 Cor. 9:24; Heb. 12:1).

What do we do with our fruit? We offer it up to the Lord. "God, I give you praise. I give you glory. I give you honor."

Look at what the apostle Paul says in 2 Timothy chapter 4 verses 6 and 7: "For I am already being poured out as a drink offering, and the time of my departure is at hand. I have fought the good fight, I have finished the race, I have kept the faith."

Isn't that a great statement? When it is time to go, don't you want to say, "I did everything He said. I am ready. I have been fruitful. And I give you all the glory and all the honor in my fruitfulness. The time of my departure is at hand, and I am ready to go. Because I have finished the course"?

In John 17 (NKJV), Jesus is praying. He says, "The hour has come. Glorify Your Son, that Your Son also may glorify You." Jesus had the most productive life of anyone who ever walked on the face of the earth.

Verse 4 says, "I glorified you on the earth." I like that. "I glorified you right where I lived. Right here. I didn't wait until I got to heaven to glorify you. I didn't wait until I got to glory to glorify you. I glorified you where I was."

You see, we must learn to glorify God by being fruitful where we are. It doesn't matter what your circumstances are. Jesus glorified God with the Roman government breathing down His neck, while His nation suffered horrible oppression. Jesus glorified Him amid a religious community that rejected Him completely and labeled Him a false prophet and a heretic. Jesus glorified God among family members who had no understanding or recognition of who He was. Among brothers who did not believe in Him and thought that He was crazy and were embarrassed by Him. Jesus glorified God surrounded by a bunch of disciples who could not seem to grasp His teachings, who kept messing up, who kept coming up with the wrong answers, who kept doubting Him, who kept telling Him what He could not do.

"How shall we feed all these people?"

Philip says, "Well, you know, we only have so much money. Send the people home."

"I did not ask you what we could not do. I said, how can we feed them?"

He glorified God in the midst of horrific abuse and torture. He prays to the Father, "I glorified your name here on the earth. Right where I live."

We are so worried about politics and taxes and laws. It doesn't make any difference who is in the White House, who is on Capitol Hill, who is in the state legislature, who is downtown at city hall. God is sovereign.

But you might argue, "Yeah, but you don't know my kids. You don't know my spouse. You don't know my situation. You don't know my finances."

Jesus said, "I glorified you in the earth. I have finished the work which you gave me to do." That God gave Him to do. He didn't do Peter's or John's work. He didn't do Paul's work. He understood what God called Him to be, and what God called Him to do, and He finished that work. He was fruitful.

He then prays, "And now, O Father, glorify Me together with Yourself, with the glory which I had with You before the world was" (verse 5).

We are blown off course so many times, we can't always say, "I have finished what you asked me to do" at this point in our lives. Each evening, we should be giving God the glory, saying, "God, I finished what you told me to do today. And, you know, it was hard."

Or maybe we're saying, "God, I finished most of what you told me to do. I got mad and blew it. Could you meet me over here in my head and get me straight, so that I can finish what you asked me to do?" It's a constant growing process.

In Acts 20:24, Paul—who had been shipwrecked, rejected, beaten, stoned, left for dead, and called a heretic—says, "But none of these things move me; nor do I count my life dear to myself, so that I might finish my race with joy, and the ministry which I received from the Lord Jesus, to testify to the gospel of the grace of God" (NKJV).

Paul says it was tough! "I have been perplexed but not rejected. I have been down but didn't quit. I have been cast aside, but I kept on. I didn't give up. I didn't grow weary in well-doing. I didn't get confused and get lost. I was determined to finish the course. I was determined to finish the purpose of God in my life. And I'm not going to die until I finish the will of God in my life."

Everybody has an appointment with death. Thank God we don't know it. "It is appointed unto man once to die, but after this the judgment" (Heb. 9:27 KJV). So we each have an appointment, but that appointment won't take place until we have done what God has designed and purposed us to do. So why worry? Just get busy doing whatever your purpose is! Do it! And be fruitful. Fulfill your ordination. You have been ordained to bring forth fruit.

Don't let anything move you. Don't let any circumstance or any person or any bad time or any economic wave move you. Just finish your course. How? With joy. Paul said, "I finished with joy, and I completed the ministry that I received, that was given to me by the Lord Jesus. I finished it."

Don't worry. You will not die before your time. You are going to fulfill everything that God has intended for you.

The Sixth "P" – Praise

Once we understand our identity in Christ and our position in Him, He reveals His purpose. Then, by his spirit, He gives us the wisdom and strength to perform the role He has laid out for us. In turn, our actions produce a product, which, in turn, gives God praise.

Chapter 11: The Praises Go Up

We've looked at the first five "P's" of our divine design. Our *Person*—we are identified by Him. Our *Position*—where we are in Him and in relation to Him. Out of that relationship, He reveals to us our *Purpose*. Then, by his spirit, He gives us the strength and the wherewithal to *Perform* our purpose. Our purpose brings forth a *Product*, which is fruit, and that fruit does something—it glorifies the Father. And that, in turn, gives Him the *Praise*.

The work in progress may seem confusing, but the end product has meaning and purpose. What's the meaning and purpose? To glorify God. That is the purpose.

We may not understand what we are going through; we may not get why we're experiencing all the trouble coming our way; we may not understand what He is doing when He is squeezing us and molding and shaping us and setting us over there, causing us to go through difficult things. But the end product, even though it may seem confusing now, has purpose and meaning, and that's to glorify God.

"By this is my Father glorified: that you bear much fruit." Your product will produce and create praise. We look at ourselves and say, "You know, I can't take any credit for this. I have to give God the glory. Oh, look at that fruitful life! Look at that wonderful marriage! Look at that relationship between that father and son! Look at that friendship! Look at that production on the job! To God be the glory!"

God gets praise; God gets honor; God gets glorified.

The greatest thing you can say when someone compliments you when you've done something well is simply this: "Thank you." Then, when you're at home, at night, get alone with the Lord and say, "God, for every pat on the back I got, for every 'job well done,' for everyone that gave me a compliment today—you know what, God? I give you all of the glory. All of the praise. All of the honor."

To praise God means to exalt Him. To extol Him. To worship Him. It is the true expression of your esteem for God.

There is a process for our praise, and there is a process for our glorifying God. Proverbs 27:21 (NKJV) says this: "As the [re]fining pot for silver, and the furnace for gold, so is a man to his praise."

What is the purpose of the refining pot; what is the purpose of the furnace? Gold is purified; silver is purified. You put the silver or gold in the vat. You turn up the degrees on the fire or the furnace, and at every so many degrees, the dross of one of the metals floats to the top. So at one temperature, all the copper dross floats to the surface. Maybe at a little higher temperature all the nickel dross floats to the top. A bit hotter, then all of the iron dross floats to the top.

Eventually all the ore floats to the top. The refiner skims off the dross in order to end up with a pure metal.

In Malachi 3:3, God is likened to a refiner's fire, sitting as a refiner of his people. To what end? "That they may offer to the Lord an offering in righteousness" (NKJV).

How does a refiner know when the gold is pure, free of all the impure metal dross? When he can look into the vat and see his reflection undistorted.

If God is our refiner, and we are perfecting our praise, when He looks into our lives, He should see no distortion. Our praise, like refined gold or silver, should mirror Jesus. Anybody got a long way to go? Yikes!

That fire gets heated up in a lot of ways. Trials and tribulations bring fire. But also praise and worship bring fire. We are purified as we worship the Lord, but trials come. You never know what is in you until someone steps on you. You never know what is in you until you get pushed or bumped the wrong way. You never know what you bleed until you are cut. And so, as the dross floats to the surface, you don't need to be embarrassed. You say, "Oh, God, I didn't recognize that was still in me." Don't go rebuking the Devil; that was you. Say, "I didn't know that was in me. Please, forgive me and deliver me from this."

See, God's purpose and our purpose are in line. Zephaniah 3:16–17 (NKJV) says: "In that day, it shall be said to Jerusalem, 'Do not fear, Zion; let not your hands be weak. The Lord your God in your midst, the Mighty One, will save; He will rejoice over you with gladness, He will quiet you with his love, He will rejoice over you with singing.'" Isn't that amazing? God singing over us?

Verse 20 then says, "At that time I will bring you back, Even at the time I gather you." In the King James version it says, "I will make you a praise among all people of the earth, when I turn back your captivity before your eyes, saith the Lord." The New King James version puts it this way: "I will give you fame and praise." But what it literally says is, "I will make *you* a praise."

God Wants You to Be a Praise

God's purpose is to make you a praise. Not to get praise out of you but to make your life a praise so people see your fruitfulness, they see your purpose being accomplished, and they see your good works and then glorify the Father, who is in heaven. He wants to make you a praise.

Remember in John 4:23 what Jesus says about worship? "The true worshippers shall worship the Father in spirit and in truth: for the Father seeketh such to worship him" (KJV). He is not seeking worship; He is seeking worshippers. He is not seeking your praise; He is desiring that you become a praise to Him.

Our product, our fruit, glorifies God. More than just the fruit of our lips. More than just the upraising of our hands. Our lives must glorify Him. That is the praise that God is after. How much more valuable is the worshipper who is fulfilling the purpose of God in her life than one who lifts her hands and offers up a sacrifice of praise, singing and worshiping, but hasn't accomplished anything for God, producing no fruit, and doesn't know her purpose?

In Genesis 4:3–5 (NKJV), we learn an interesting fact about worship. It says, "In the process of time it came to pass that Cain brought an offering of fruit of the ground to the Lord. Abel also brought of the firstborn of his flock and of their fat. And the Lord respected Abel and his offering. But He did not respect Cain and his offering. Cain was very angry, and his countenance fell."

Isn't it interesting that the issue regarding the sacrifice was one of respect? Does God respect your life? Because He respected Abel's life, He respected his offering. Because He did not respect Cain's life, He did not receive Cain's offering. It didn't mean that He did not love Cain. He later came to Cain and said, in essence, "Listen, sin is crouching at the door. If you do right, everything will be all right" (Gen. 4:6, 7). He still loved Cain; He did not destroy him after he killed Abel. He sent him off to the land of Nod and marked his forehead to keep him safe.

God's desire is to restore us, but I wonder if God can respect our lives. What kind of life does God respect? A life that is productive.

Remember, He gives us the purpose, He gives us the gifts, He gives us the talents, and then He gives us the Holy Spirit to empower us to do the work, and He gets the glory and we get the blessing of being co-laborers with Him.

So, when God desires to make you a praise, it is His desire to make your *life* a praise. Ephesians 1:12 (NKJV) says that "we who first trusted in Christ should be to the praise of His glory." Our purpose is to be a praise. We are not just to give praise, to offer praise with our mouths and our uplifted hands.

Hebrews 13:15 says, "For by him let us offer a sacrifice of praise to God continually." Praise is not something that we just give. It is something that we are. And it is a result of our life and our relationship with God. We are esteeming Him.

How do we, then, offer continually a sacrifice of praise? By living lives that are productive. You get up early and you begin worshiping the Lord. You wake up late at night and can't sleep, so you give God praise. You are on the job and you step into the restroom because you need a break, and you say, "Oh, I just thank you, Lord." It is inclusive of those things, but it is not limited to them.

Psalm 119:164 says, "Seven times a day, I will praise you." Remember the seven pillars that make up who we are? In all those areas, we should be a praise to God.

It is kind of tough for you to be praising God and owing somebody some money who is sitting right next to you in the sanctuary. How can you be praising God in church while that person is thinking, "I wish they'd pay me my money. I wish they'd ask forgiveness for the way they treated me. I forgive them. But, gee, I wish they hadn't been so mean. I wish I hadn't seen them fighting over that parking space out on the lot. About to get in a fistfight. I wish I hadn't heard them in the restroom gossiping about that poor lady whose shoes don't match her dress."

Psalm 50:23 says, "Whosoever offers praise glorifies me." When you offer praise, you are giving God the full honor. That offering is not just with the mouth, the clapping or raising of the hands, or the dancing of our feet.

I think Jesus whittled it down when He urged his followers, "You really want to know how to glorify the Father? Let's cut to the chase: be productive in your life. And God will be glorified. Go and bear much fruit. You know what? Then you will ask the Father in my name, and you know what He will do? He will give it to you. It's tied to that."

Dr. Tony Williams

The Seventh "P" – Presence

*Lives that are in line with God's purpose produce praise, and that ushers us into God's presence—
the place we always want to be.*

Chapter 12: Oh, to Be in His Presence

Our product will produce and create a praise. Which brings us to the place we have been trying to get to. This is our reward. This is our goal. This is what our Christian life is about. This is where we abide. This is where we live, move, and have our being. His presence. I have a saying that I love: "God is as near as a whispered prayer." He is just that near. I want His presence.

When I first got saved, I didn't go into the ministry. I didn't become a Christian to preach. I didn't even know anything about preaching. When I got saved, it was because I loved Jesus. Because He delivered me from my purposeless life, and all I wanted to do was just be with Him. Then, as I got involved with the church and went deep into my study of the Bible, I found that God had bigger things in store for me. But I never forget his calling—which is to be with Him. That is what we are in pursuit of.

Nothing else can take the place of the presence of God. If God does not show up, we have wasted our time. If we do not learn how to wait on Him, we have missed the essence of the joy of our salvation. And that is the abiding in His presence. The presence of God does not come by skill or talent. It does not come by contrivance or performance of some ritual. The presence of God comes through praise and worship. It is the result of a productive life, a fruitful life. Psalm 22:3 (NKJV) says, "But you are holy, enthroned in the praises of Israel."

We are in desperate need of the presence of God. We need Him in our lives at every level, in every nook and corner. In Genesis 28:15, God makes this promise to Jacob: "I am with you and will watch over you wherever you go" (NIV). No matter where we are, we should be able to have a sense of the presence of God.

I remember one time when my oldest daughter got in trouble at high school, and I had to go sit in the principal's office, and I was really mad. And what made me madder was she was not talking. You know how teenagers are? I asked her, "Well, why would you do that?" Silence. I wanted to leap over and choke her. "Speak up!" I was so embarrassed. She was not saying anything. "Uh, I don't know. Uh."

As I fumed, I thought, "You know what? I need God's presence right here in the principal's office, where I'm about to blow up. Let me sense you here with me in this." Instantly, I got a sense of the presence of God. I didn't have any warm feeling or hear any words. I just sensed the sweet presence of God in a way that calmed my spirit and my heart. I told God, "You are with me wherever I go. Whatever the situation, I need to recognize the presence of God."

We need God in our battles. Deuteronomy 20:1 says, "When you go out to battle against your enemies . . . the Lord your God is with you" (NKJV). So when you are battling the enemy, or battling some folks or some situations, you need the presence of the Lord with you.

In all our trials, He has promised to be with us. Isaiah 43:2 tells us that God will be with us when we go through the water and through the fire.

What a promise. Jesus says God's presence will be with us "even to the ends of the earth," or "to the end of the age," as some translations put it. And we are reassured in Hebrews 13:5 that God will never leave or forsake us.

God's Presence in Our Lives

As our product produces praise, our praise provides entrance for the presence of God in our lives. There are various aspects of the presence of God. First, there is *omnipresence*. That means He is everywhere. Everywhere we go.

We also have His *abiding* presence. That means that He is *within* me. He lives in me. He has taken up His abode on the throne of my heart, always present, all the time.

Then there is His *manifest* presence—His revealing presence that is overwhelming. Have you ever been in the presence of God in such a way that you either wept or felt utterly peaceful? Or in a worship service when the presence of God is powerful?

God is always in the right place. He is always the Lord God. We put Him in the right place in relationship to our lives. We put Him on the throne. The psalmist says in Psalm 99:5: "Exalt the Lord our God and worship at his footstool" (NIV). You exalt the Lord. You get Him enthroned in the right place in your life. High and lifted up. And then you get in your place. You got God in his place; now you get in your place. Where is your place? At his feet. At his footstool. That is your place.

When you get in your place and honor God in His place, anything can happen. God does the most impossible things. He splits Red Seas. He puts air-conditioning in fiery furnaces. He makes lions lose their appetites. He raises the dead. If you have God continually in His right place, where you worship at His footstool, anything can happen.

Psalm 100 speaks of our entrance into His presence. "Come before his presence." How do you come before His presence? With singing. "Enter into His gates with thanksgiving, And into His courts with praise" (NKJV). Our entrance into his presence is with worship and singing and praise.

When our lives are fruitful, and when we are giving worship and praise as a result of that productive life, praise leads us from self-centeredness to an awareness of the presence of God. God is always there. We are just too busy to notice. We are just too busy to stop and sense His presence.

In Exodus 33:12–13 (NKJV), Moses is having his conversation with the Lord.

> Then Moses said to the Lord, "See, You say to me, 'bring up this people.' But You have not let me know whom You will send with me. Yet You have said, 'I know you by name, and you also have found grace in My sight.' Now therefore, I pray, if I have found grace in Your sight, show me now Your way, that I may know You, and that I might find grace in Your sight. And consider this nation is Your people."

Moses essentially says to God, "If your presence isn't going with us, don't bring us up from here." In other words, "If you're not going, forget it. I'm not going." Moses valued God's presence more than he valued His promise.

There's a story of a little boy who won a sixty-second shopping spree at Toys-R-Us. He was given one minute, and everything he could grab and carry over the finish line would be his. So his brothers and sisters, friends, and family coached him all week. "Head for the video games. They cost a lot. Fill the cart with video games, grab a bicycle, and drag it on back."

On the morning of the event he first walked the aisles to look at all the toys. Then he waited with his cart as the countdown began. 5-4-3-2-1. *Ring!* As the clock ticked the time, the boy froze. Fifteen seconds passed. Thirty seconds passed. He couldn't think of what to grab. Everyone was yelling, "Go, just go get something! Just get anything! Go!" His family cheered and urged him on.

Forty-five seconds passed, and then he spotted the owner of the store. He raced with his basket down that aisle, knocked the man into the basket, turned around, and crossed the finish line just in time.

The owner stared at him from the cart, confused. "Why did you do that?" he asked.

The boy, panting, out of breath, said, "If I got you, I got everything in here."

If We Have God, We Have Everything

And so it is with God. Why would we seek after temporal, material things? If I've got God, I've got everything I need. There is no lack. There is no deficit. There is nothing missing when I have God. In the presence of the Lord, there is fullness.

King David was in continual pursuit of the presence of God, even when he made mistakes. "Cast me not away from thy presence; and take not thy holy spirit from me. Restore unto me the joy of thy salvation." (Psalm 51:11–12 KJV).

God's design for our lives is to bring us into His presence, and when we are in His presence, being fruitful and productive, we bring glory and honor to Him. Psalm 40:13 says, "The upright shall dwell in your presence." It is our dwelling place. It is where we belong. The upright live there. They abide there. They take up and make their house there in His presence. Psalm 16:11 (KJV) says, "In thy presence there is fullness of joy." His presence becomes for us the place of fulfillment. It is the place of His provision and the place of His power.

In His presence, there is absolute fullness. No lack. First Chronicles 16:27 says, "Honor and glory are in his presence." The place of our honor, where we are honored, is in His presence. Remember, Jesus said, "Why do you seek honor from one another and not from the only one who really counts?" And that is God.

You are not going to find honor trying to get a pat on the back from people. You want to be honored? Get in the presence of the Lord. He will honor you with His mercy. He will honor you with His grace. He will honor you with forgiveness. He will honor you with His loving-kindness. He will honor you with His love. He will honor you with His power. He will honor your with His comfort. He will honor you with His peace. He will honor you with His joy. He will honor you, if you will just get in His presence. Exalt Him, and rush to your place—at His feet.

Mary, wanting to be with Jesus, was found at His feet. Jesus said, "She has chosen that good part." That was no way a slam on Martha at all. But Mary had chosen the good part, "and that will not be taken away from her" (Luke 10:42 NKJV).

Did Martha need to be rattling the pots and the pans? Sure she did. Somebody had to cook. You cannot live on prayer alone. Do we need to serve the Lord? Absolutely. Did Martha need to be in the kitchen? Absolutely. But you cannot be there all the time. It wasn't a knock on Martha; it was a praise of Mary, telling her that her service honored and glorified God.

Jude 24 (KJV) says, "Now unto him that is able to keep you from falling." Jesus is able to keep you. And not only is he able to keep you from falling, He is able to "present you faultless." With all the bad things we have done, all the shortcomings, all the mistakes, I scratch my head at this. He is going to present me faultless? I have blown it so many times. I have made so many mistakes. But He is going to present me faultless. Where is He going to present me? Before God's presence. The presence of His glory. And do you know what else? He is going to do it with "exceeding joy." He is going to be glad to do it.

We need His help. We need His presence. We need His help to come into His presence. But His presence is where He designed us to be. His presence is what we are after.

Made for His Purpose

We are made for His purpose. We are divinely designed.

First, He identifies us. We learn who He is and who we are. We then recognize where we are, what our position must be, in relation to His position. When we are honest with Him, He will meet us there. In His presence, that's where He will unfold to us our purpose, our destiny.

We must then work out our own salvation; we must perform the purpose of God that He has given to us. That performance will bring about a product, or fruit, that which we produce. And, in turn, our fruit produces praise. The presence of God then comes and inhabits our praises. And that is what we all need—the continual, abiding presence of God. God continually being honored and glorified in our lives. Not because we are merely saying, "Praise God, praise God, praise God," but because our lives are a praise to His glory, and our lives offer to Him continually a sacrifice of praise.

We must continually be moving forward in the purposes of God for our lives, and we must continually be abiding in Him because He adjusts our purpose along the way. What my purpose was in God twenty-five years ago is not my purpose in God today. It is incorporated and part of the learning process and part of who I am, but my purposes have changed.

God wants us to continually grow. If we stay stuck in one place, then there is no stretching. God wants to stretch us. Why? So we can contain more of Him. So our capacity to receive from Him is increased. He stretches us so that we can contain more of His purpose and more of His will.

You are made for His purpose! By understanding the "Seven P's" of your divine design, you can find your place, position yourself in His presence, and be a praise to Him now and forever. Amen!

About the Author

Dr. Tony Williams has served as senior pastor of Maranatha Christian Center in San Jose, California, since 1987. In 2001, he was appointed chairman of the board for Cityteam Ministry's International Committee. He is a volunteer chaplain at the Santa Clara County jail, as well as for the San Jose Police Department and volunteers at San Quentin prison.

His missionary work has taken him all over the world—from Mexico to East Africa, from the Fiji Islands to Dublin, Ireland, and numerous locales in between.

Pastor Tony currently serves on the board of directors for Cityteam Ministries. Previously he has served as a board member for the Coalition for Urban Youth Leadership, Fellowship West, Inc. (Los Angeles), and the Bay Area Billy Graham Crusade.

Dr. Williams earned a bachelor of theology from California Graduate School of Theology in Glendale, California; a master's degree in ministry and honorary doctorate of divinity from Southern California School of Ministry; a doctor of humane letters and a doctor of philosophy in Christian counseling from Vision International University.

www.ingramcontent.com/pod-product-compliance
Lightning Source LLC
Chambersburg PA
CBHW071300040426
42444CB00009B/1803